WHO TOOK THE BIT OUT OF THE HORSE'S MOUTH

MOTHER NAVADIA MOORE
BISHOP LEROY C.E. NEWMAN

eta Publishing

Ocala, FL

Copyright © 2018 Leroy Newman

All rights reserved. No part of this publication may be reproduced, distributed, or transmitted in any form or by any means, including photocopying, recording, or other electronic or mechanical methods, without the prior written permission of the publisher, except in the case of brief quotations embodied in critical reviews and certain other noncommercial uses permitted by copyright law. For permission requests, write to the publisher, addressed "Attention: Permissions Coordinator," at the address below.

Zeta Publishing, Inc
3850 SE 58th Ave
Ocala, FL 34480
www.zetapublishing.com

Scripture quotations marked KJV are from the Holy Bible, King James Version (Authorized Version. First published in 1611. Quotes from the KJV classic Reference Bible, Copyright 1983 by The Zondervan Corporation.

Ordering Information:
Quantity sales. Special discounts are available on quantity purchases by corporations, associations, and others. For details, contact the publisher at the address above.
Orders by U.S. trade bookstores and wholesalers. Please contact Zeta Publishing: Tel: (352) 694-2553; Fax: (352) 694-1791 or visit www.zetapublishing.com

ISBN: 978-1-947191-60-0 (sc)
ISBN: 978-1-947191-61-7 (e)

Library of Congress: 2017964672
Printed in the United States of America

Table of Contents

Focus 1

Forward 3

Introduction 7

Section One

1. The Bit 13

2. The Bitting Process 25

3. The Wall of Resistance 35

4. Seeds That Bitting Produce 49

Section Two

5. Christ's Second Coming 57

6. Barriers To Responsibility 65

7. Obedience 73

8. The Mouth 85

9. Prayerfulness 91

10. Leadership 101

Section Three

11. Servant Leadership Traits 115

12. Profiles of Highly Effective Servant Leaders 121

13. Make a Difference 133

14. The Called 139

15. Humility 145

Section Four

16. The Anointing 165

17. The Secret Anointing 169

18. Moving Outside Your Comfort Zone 175

19. Today's Servant Leader 179

20. Tomorrow's Servant Leaders 183

21. Yesterday's Servant Leaders 189

FOCUS ON THE TEXT

Too many believers in ministry have failed to step into their purpose because of a lack of knowledge and a lack of discipline. Launching a ministry into one's Divine Purpose requires focus on vision and a commitment, dedication, and devotion to visionary purpose.

FORWARD

This book is as much about leadership as it is about guidance and discipleship. When James, in the third chapter used the bit and bridle to allegorize the controlling of the believers, he gave much thought to his choice of objects. Although the reader is drawn to focus on the believer's attitude toward ministry, much consideration must be given to the master of the beast who holds the reins of the bridle that contains the bit. His ability to discern the need and purpose for bridling is most important, as is the level of governance the believer requires in developing his or her character. I speak as one who has been under pastoral leadership from a child. I can almost say that I was born in ministry because my parents were believers filled with the Holy Ghost in a local Pentecostal (sanctified) church. It is the pastor who is responsible for the teaching and nurturing of the church. I grew up before this so call new

Christian enlightenment or contemporary church area. My pastors perhaps did not go to a renowned seminary, but they prayed a lot and heard from God as to how to lead the people of God. Their reins were the word of God.

Properly used, the Word of God can pull, push, and turn us in every direction possible. The reins of the Gospel can be used to drive ambitious believers to new dominions and prevent the over-zealous from falling into the pit of despair. Those of us who were raised on the farm understand the importance of the bit and reins on the bridle. One of the interesting things about the reins is they are not only used to drive the horse or mule they are also used to tie them in a certain place. While being tied to a post they are fed special foods and not allowed to roam around eating what they want.

Too often does the glamour of ministry lead to over zealousness and unharnessed ambitions. When commitment is rewarded with assignment and vision, it must be tempered with reasonable service, stewardship, and preparation. Before birthing there must be a period of gestation, prenatal care, and labor. Submission to the bitting process requires that the visionary trust leadership. During this process a period of self-examination may be required; however, it is not easy to turn the spotlight inward upon one's self. Pastors are required to test the commitment of those over which they have been given oversight.

Pastors are not moved by the giftedness or the liberality of the believer; they are overseers and stewards of another man's heritage. Too many times ministries are held hostage by the gifted and the liberal who feel that they should have ministerial privileges because of their gifts. There must be integrity in ministry, both from the perspective of the leadership and from the fellowship. However, in today's society, and I regret to say in the church, integrity seems to retreat into a dark closet, and wicked things that were hidden in the closet have come out into the open. The church is faced with compromise, tolerance, and spiritual weaknesses that have driven many of today's believers into a massive peril of evil. Today's church desperately need believers with integrity, ethics, and commitment who will stand on the principles of the gospel and true Holiness regardless of the cost.

It is time for a revival of integrity, conviction, commitment, dedication, and devotion. It must begin with the leadership of the church: the Pastor, the Elders, the Mothers, and all who are connected to the leadership. At home fathers need to be men of integrity; mothers, women of virtue. Husbands need to set good examples for their children and for their wives. Grandparents must also be godly in their relationships with their grandchildren. Ethics and godly principles must be the cornerstone of every believer's character. All who are in leadership, both secular and spiritual, must manifest the highest level of integrity possible.

INTRODUCTION

Being raised by my grandparents who were sharecroppers on a south Florida truck farm, I know something about bridles and bits. It was almost impossible in the late 50's and 60's to bring in a crop or even plough a field without the use of a mule or horse. The one thing that gave the ploughmen power over the mule was the bridle, its bit, and rein. The ploughman could determine the direction of the mule or horse or oxen or in other parts of the country, the reindeer or caribou from the back of the animal or from the front. He could even guide the animal from the side. The one thing that made it possible was the bridle and bit.

For more than 6,000 years or so man has been using bits in the mouths of animal (mostly horses and mules) to control their directions. However, these animals have not always responded well to the process. Their objections are understandable considering that the wrong bits, or bits in the wrong mouths or in the wrong hands do inflict pain on a very sensitive part of the anatomy. You may ask, why not use a bitless bridle. Bitless bridles, which have equally ancient roots, provide alternative means of influencing the speed and direction of horses without risking oral pain and the resistance that arise from it.

The bitting process that James speaks about is important to the development of a believer's character. However, discipline in the hands of the wrong leader can be as damaging to a believer as putting the wrong bit in a horse's mouth. Those of us who grew up around horses and mules know that there are different types of bits, depending upon the character and personality of the horse.

Scripture tells us to, "Know them that labor among you." Every leader must know character and disposition of his or her followers, especially those who are being discipled by them. The process of bitting varies from believer to believer. Some may require vigorous bitting while others may only need gentle guidance. Others may not require bitting at all, but keep in mind that bitless bridling can be as painful and dangerous as bitted bridling. Bitless bridles can create a false sense of liberty, and as leaders in ministry the least thing a leader needs is a disciple who feel he or she can go or do as he or she pleases; I have always felt that no matter what level of maturity a believer is, there should be some form of governing the development of his or her Christian character. There is a certain psychology that develops along with one's character, and bitting increases the likelihood that a disciple will question his or her actions before they commit to them.

Keep in mind that un-bitted horses and mules don't run free; they are corralled or allowed to roam within a fenced area. Good leaders are always mindful of the danger posed by unguarded sheep. Even when all is done to protect those whom the Lord has entrusted to us we sometime fail. If you are under the leadership of God's workman, submit to the bitting process. And watch how your character develops and how you mature.

SECTION ONE

CHAPTER ONE

THE BIT

The bit is a restraining device used by equestrians (horsemen) to communicate their will with the horse upon which they are riding; the bit is placed in the interdental region of the mouth where there are no teeth. It is held in the horse's mouth by a bridle that is fitted with reins that are attached to it by which the rider controls the direction of the horse. If Paul had listed the "bit" as a part of the Christian's armor, the "bit" would be listed somewhere between the "helmet of salvation" and the "breastplate of righteousness." As believers we are admonished in regards to our disposition not to be as horses and mules, which require bridles and bits to control the direction in which we go.

> *Be ye not as the horse or as the mule, which have no understanding; whose mouth must be held in with bit and bridle...*
> *Psalm 32:9*

There are different types of bridles and bits that are suited for the horse in accordance to its character or maturity. Some horses do not require the use of a bit, but are controlled with the reins of a bitless bridle. James used the bit and bridle as metaphors that represent the guidance of the Holy Spirit when he was faced with teaching members of the newly formed church about the control of the tongue.

There appears to have been members in the congregation who were gifted with oratorical abilities, and because of this, felt that they were qualified to be teachers in the church. James replied by saying, teaching requires more than the ability to read and speak eloquently; it requires restraint. You can't just say what you want to say or do what you feel should be done as a course of action. As visionaries, we get our directions from God and impart only what is divinely mandated by Him.

> *My son, despise not thou the chastening (guidance) of the Lord, nor faint when thou art rebuked of him: For whom the Lord loveth he chasteneth, and scourgeth every son whom he receiveth*
> *Hebrews 12:5-6*

We are not our own; neither are we lords over them whom the Lord has given us rule. As visionary leaders, we are responsible for the believer's growth and development as Christians. I must admit there is a problem in the church with leadership. There are too many believers operating as visionaries independently of leadership and oversight, saying and doing as they please. Not only have they not been submissive to the "bitting process," many of them have never been "bridled." God has no respect of person; all must submit to the Will of God and walk worthy of the vocation wherein they are called. No one is exempt from the chastening of God, neither male nor female, preacher nor teacher, believer nor non-believer. The "bitting process" makes all worthy of the vocation.

> *Behold, we put bits in the horses' mouths, that they may obey us; and we turn about their whole body. James 3:3*

Spiritually, the bit controls, sharpens, molds, and directs the path of the believer. It promotes spiritual maturity that enhances Christian development, increases wisdom, knowledge, and enlightenment that ultimately lead to elevation and promotion.

Revealed things are taught by the Holy Spirit

> *When we tell you these things, we do not use words that come from human wisdom. Instead, we speak words given to us by the Spirit, using the Spirit's words to explain spiritual truths*
> *I Corinthians 2:13*

> **Submission to the bitting process enhances personal development and Christian character. It increases one's commitment, dedication, and devotion to the work of ministry.**

No visionary is elevated to an office of leadership knowing all there is to know about the office to which he or she is promoted. There is a period of preparation and a process of validation that must take place. Scripture says, "lean not to thine own understanding, in all thy ways acknowledge him, and he shall direct thy paths." The tenacity of bitting and the persistence associated with its guidance, forces the believer to focus on the development of his or her personal ministries and the consistent self-evaluation of his or her Christian character. Bitting removes the likelihood of developing an atmosphere of envy and strife among believers as well as prevents creating the spirit of backbiting which almost always emerges out of confusion.

Visionary leaders must identify those within the congregation who have attached themselves to the ministry but who themselves need bridling, and determine what level of restraint is required.

Some form of bridling is required for all believers, but not all need bitting. Christian development and spiritual maturity mandates the need for control. Visionary leaders must identify those within the congregation who have attached themselves to their ministries but who themselves need bridling, and determine what level of restraint is required. Those who have devoted much time and energy to Christian education and have been rewarded for their academic achievement may only need a bridle without the bit. Remember, the bridle is designed to mandate control and communication through the use of the reins attached to it. Those who can minister within the boundaries of the visionary leader may not need the bit in their mouths to keep them under control because they are submissive to the Holy Spirit, which they have allowed to take rule of their lives.

Just as there are different bits for different personalities in a horse's behavior, there are different requirements for believers at different levels of their Christian maturity.

There is an array of reasons that may mandate the use of the bit in the mouth of a believer. Some of which include, but is not limited to, a lack of Christian development and spiritual maturity, over zealousness, insensitivity to needs, intemperance, and lack of prayer in the life of believers. Just as there are different bits for different personalities in a horse's behavior, there are different requirements for believers at different levels of their Christian maturity. One believer may only require counseling while another may require chaperoning. Different levels of zealousness may mandate different approaches by leadership as the believer moves toward fulfilling his or her calling. The Elder, the Minister, the Prophet, the Evangelist all may be working toward the same visionary reality, but under different leadership supervision. James also associates the bridle with self-governance: "if one can bridle his tongue he is able to control his whole body." The tongue, though very small, has a profound effect on a person's character and how he or she is perceived. Those who cannot bridle themselves need the oversight of leadership. The horse with an aggressive nature has but one goal and that is to run the race. He stands at the gate, prancing and neighing, and is held back only by pulling on the rein which applies pressure to the bit in his mouth. Keeping a tight rein on the method, in which ministers approach the development of their ministries, will control the aggressive nature of some believers. They must be nurtured and tutored to become more temperate and gentle and loving in spirit while at the same time be persuasive in proclaiming God's will.

The bit is not a weapon nor is it an instrument of chastisement.

Where there is no oversight of ministry there is a danger of scattering the sheep and hindering the process that bring reality to visionary purpose. Have you ever noticed that as a child matures, the less it wants the parent to hold its hand when crossing the street? So it is with some believers, the more they learn, the more they desire independence. Without relinquishing oversight, it is the responsibility of the visionary leader to discern at what stage in ministry or at what level of maturity to let go. The bit is not a weapon nor is it an instrument of chastisement. It helps however in governing the potential of the believer and guards the integrity of his or her ministry. One can only develop into a strong leader who will confront, correct, and encourage God's people after he or she has been submissive to the chastening of the Lord.

In the early church the pastor kept strict oversight over the members of the fellowship. One might say, too strict an oversight. We couldn't visit other churches without permission; we couldn't wear certain clothing, play certain games or eat certain foods. We were compelled to come to prayer service, go on fasts, be in Sunday school and participate in almost every church function. If we didn't, we had to give account as to why. One could say that there was too much oversight; but as it was, it fostered a strong foundation on which the believer could stand, build ministries and develop vision. In hindsight, we could have gone to a ball game and still have been saved or eaten certain foods and not have jeopardized our salvation. By today's standards, we could have been saved without tarrying. However, those prohibitions did not harm, but instead gave depth to our spiritual maturity. Pastors guarded the faith with what God gave them in their season of administration and oversight. The strict oversight of our early church fathers was a way of keeping the bit in the horses' mouth and holding a tight rein over their ministries.

The question of who took the bit out of the horse's mouth is a perplexing one; no pastor will admit the blame. It is a combination of the accessibility to religious education and ministerial ambition. The increase in the number of ministries operating today and the number of young believers entering the ministry has added to the problem. As unbelievable as it may seem, there are ministers, pastors, prophets, apostles and even bishops who are functioning as visionary leaders, and who themselves have not been called or consecrated to these offices. They are teaching erroneous doctrines and allowing unholy practices to be committed in their churches. At best they are lukewarm and out of compliance with the Will of God. Research shows that many of these "bastard" leaders have un-teachable spirits and were unable to submit to the leadership of their former pastors (leaders).

> *Godly leadership is tantamount to Godly stewardship; if you cannot grasp the art of "follow-ship," you most likely cannot become a visionary leader.*

The author of the Gospel of John, chapter nine, in dealing with the character of the Pharisees came to the conclusion that they had un-teachable spirits. They were arrogant, obnoxious, callous, and haughty. The un-teachable, like the Pharisees, think they know more than others; they themselves are teachers, but think they need no teaching. They promote their own agenda and are critics of others. They look down on anyone who does not belong to their group and insist their opinion is to be considered or none at all. However, the visionary leader must be a servant first, then a disciple willing to learn and have a disposition void of harmful Pharisaic characteristics. Godly leadership is tantamount to Godly stewardship; if you cannot grasp the art of "follow-ship," you most likely cannot become a visionary leader.

The Shepherd knows his sheep, and communicates with them, but it is just as important for the sheep to know the Shepherd. "My sheep know my voice, and I know them, and they follow me." (John 10:27) Each sheep has its own personality, and yet as different as they are, the visionary leader must through ministry, find a way to bring each of them to a new dimension of faith and obedience to God.

> *All scripture is given by the inspiration of God and is profitable for doctrine, for reproof, for correction, for instruction in righteousness: That the man of God may be perfect, thoroughly furnished unto all good works;*
> *II Timothy 3:16-17*

Seasoned leaders are team builders and use the "bitting" of the believer to promote unity within the confines of ministry

Seasoned leaders hone or sharpen their leadership skills so that they may communicate with the entire community of believers whether they are ready to hear or not, whether they are ready to obey or not, and whether they are ready to submit to bitting or not. Seasoned leaders are team builders and use the "bitting" of the believer to promote unity within the confines of ministry so that the believer may persevere in spite of opposition to his or her individual and personal development. Paul writes to the Corinthians….

> *I am made all things to all men that I might by all means save some.*
> *I Corinthians 9:22*

After the believer has submitted to his or her season of bitting, the walk with

the Lord becomes a walk of faith and justification.

After the horse has submitted to the control of the bit, it does not see the bit as an instrument of discipline and control but as a tool by which his master (the horseman) communicates his desires hopes and aspirations to him. The bit in due season, teaches the horse to trust his master and believe in the directions administered. Therefore, the offences and oppositions of the enemy that waits in the path that the visionary has laid do not affect the reality of the visionary's predestined purpose. After the believer has submitted to his or her season of bitting, the walk with the Lord becomes a walk of faith and justification.

Those who have endured their season of bitting have developed the grace to bridle their tongues and demonstrate a high level of restraint.

Paul, grieved in spirit with the church of Corinth because of their lack of spiritual maturity and Christian development in relations to their personal ministries, spoke to them with seasoned words and referred to them as stewards and believers while at the same time sharing with them his disenchantment with their perception of his authority as visionary and overseer of the church. As servants of Christ Jesus, our ministries may take us into unfamiliar territories; we may find ourselves caught up emotionally in visions orchestrated by the ambition of man and not of God. It is at this time that the visionary under whose oversight we have been placed pulls the rein that applies pressure to the bit in our spiritual mouths. Those who have endured their season of bitting have developed the grace to bridle their tongues and to demonstrate a high level of restraint. This puts us back on the path that the Lord has given for us to follow.

Bitting fosters humility and meekness as well as unity among the saints.

Paul, while addressing the Corinthian church, could have boasted of his office as an Apostle. He could have rehearsed with them his resume of accomplishments or even bragged of his experiences with God in the desert of Arabia. However, he chose to remind them that he was only a servant, a minister of the mysteries of God even a prisoner of the gospel of Jesus Christ. Bitting fosters humility and meekness as well as unity among the saints. It governs the tongue and prevents one from offending his brother with words; for this is the mark of a perfect man.

> *If any man offend not in word the same is a perfect man, and able also to bridle the whole body. Behold, we put bits in the horses' mouths that they may obey us; and we turn about their whole body. But the tongue can no man tame; it is an unruly evil, full of deadly poison. Out of the same mouth proceedeth blessing and cursing. My brethren, theses things ought not so to be.*
> *James 3:2-3, 8, 10*

Those who fail to become submissive to the bitting process will ultimately become unruly, un-teachable, and unfaithful.

Bits are not only used to guide one in a certain direction or in a particular path that has already been laid, but they also give one access to new dimensions of ministry. Somewhat like the bit that is used in construction, which is used to cut through certain barriers or impediments to allow accessibility, the bitting process cuts through insensitivity and intemperance. As a parallel point of reference, submission to the bitting process enhances personal development and Christian character. It increases one's commitment, dedication, and devotion toward the work of ministry. Those who fail to become submissive to the bitting process will ultimately become unruly, unteachable, and unfaithful. They become tares among wheat, and thorns in the flesh of leadership.

CHAPTER TWO

THE BITTING PROCESS

The bitting process is an ongoing process that enhances spiritual development. It is a method that proves one's worthiness and sharpens one's ability to develop relationships both spiritually and secularly. It is an ongoing process that helps in the development of a "servant heart." One cannot minister effectively without a heart for God's people. As we develop as leaders, evidence of our commitment to our visionary purpose will be revealed and we will begin see where God is taking us spiritually. Understanding your purpose is most important when embarking on new ministerial endeavors. We must believe and demonstrate that we are called for a purpose. If we can't convince ourselves of our calling, we will never be able to convince anyone else. We may have matured as a Christian and proven that we love the Lord, but as visionaries, we are novices, "babes," and may need more bitting or guidance in the development of our visionary purpose.

Paul in his writing to the Philippian Church said, *"Brethren, I count not myself to have apprehended: but this one thing I do, forgetting those things which are behind, and reaching forth toward those things which are before." (Philippians 3:13)* Paul here is saying, I have not yet attained and I'm not perfect. The most matured Christian must also be the most humble. The nearer we draw to Christ, the more we feel our own unworthiness. The more the light of Christ manifests itself in our hearts, the more we see ourselves as sinners saved by grace and understand that the seed of sin remains in our flesh, and the more we are not to yield to it, but strive after perfection. Every Christian knows his or her weaknesses. They also know that as Christians they are to trust God and lean not to their own understanding, but to acknowledge God, and He will direct their paths.

Christ is the author and finisher of our faith; He first apprehended Paul on the Damascus road. This experience was so life changing that Paul *strove* (emphasis added) to lay hold upon Christ. Therefore, because Christ first loved us, we now must love him. As believers we are to never become satisfied with ourselves or with our accomplishments, but we are to press onwards toward the mark of the higher calling. We are not to become complacent with our attainments, but as Paul said, forgetting the progress which we have made and move forward to higher heights or deeper depths.

Stepping into visionary purpose carries with it a new set of perimeters. Just as there were tests to prove our willingness to be submissive to the guidance of the Holy Spirit during the bitting process, there are tests to prove our readiness to face the challenges that opposes the reality of the vision shown to us by God. To endure the hardness of turning vision into reality one must stand on the Word of God and study to show him or herself approved. It is the Word that gets the believer from one level of ministry to the next. Understanding how God brought the prophets and the Apostles through will be invaluable in helping us make our visions reality. The Word will anchor us, give us stability and soundness; it will keep us focused and make us steadfast and unmovable. David said, *"Thy Word have I hid in my heart."* It keeps us from yielding to temptation and adds credibility and integrity to our character. It acts like a lighthouse, always pointing us to safety. David hid the Word in his heart. Jeremiah said *"I found thy words and did eat them; they were the joy and rejoicing in mine heart."* Ezekiel said the Lord commanded him to open his mouth and eat that which He give him; then he looked, and beheld a hand in front of him, and a roll of a book was therein; and He spread it before him; and it was written within and without: and there was written therein lamentations, and mourning, and woe.

The Word, when studied, prepares us for joy and rejoicing, lamentations and mourning, victories and failures. The reward is not in the test it is in how we handle the test. Do we boast over victories or do we allow defeat to destroy our determination to turn our visions into reality? Giving up is not an option for the believer. Once we are free we must stand in that liberty, and be not entangled again with the yoke of bondage. We are nurtured by the Word. We are consumed by it. It becomes our very being and our faith is established upon it. It becomes our road map: *"a lamp unto my feet."*

The Word is a bridle and bit that keeps us moving in the right direction or forces us back on the right path.

God's Word creates a humble heart, proclaims an assurance that God's blessings are laid up for the believer who submits to His guidance and trust in Him completely. It is not for one man alone or tribe or people; it is not for one nation or religion. God's Word is for, *"Whosoever will."* It is living communication directly from God to every man, woman, and child in this season and time, and times to come. The Word is a bridle and bit that keeps us moving in the right direction or forces us back on the right path. It carries with it enduring strength and power for growth and restoration for all who receive it.

> *For the word of God is quick, and powerful, and sharper than any two-edged sword, piercing even to the dividing asunder of soul and spirit, and of the joints and marrow, and is a discerner of the thoughts and intents of the heart.* (Other translations say, "The Word of God is living")
> Hebrews 4:12

The word of God is alive and active. Sharper than any double-edged sword, it penetrates even to dividing soul and spirit, joints and marrow; it judges the thoughts and attitudes of the heart. Jesus showed a link between the written Word of God and Himself, in that He is the subject of the written Word.

> *You study the Scriptures diligently because you think that in them you have eternal life. These are the very Scriptures that testify about me.*
> John 5:39

When Jesus was being tempted by Satan, He answered, *"Man does not live by bread alone, but by every word [rhema] that proceeds from the mouth of God." (Matthew 4:4)* We are told in Ephesians 6:17 to *"take the helmet of salvation and the sword of the Spirit, which is the Word [rhema] of God."* Jesus demonstrated that we need the actual recorded Words of God to overcome Satan's attacks. Rhema is Greek for "Word", often used when we refer to the spoken words of Jesus.

As we study this text and the effects of the "Word" on our lives and its importance in turning our visions into reality, it becomes the foundation upon which we build our ministries. It becomes the bit and bridle that gives obedience to our character and integrity to our calling. I can remember driving a wagon through the field and how important the bridle and reins were in controlling the horse. It did not matter what the task was: pulling the wagon, ploughing, pulling stump, or just going for a joy ride, the bridle, the reins, and bit were the most important part of preparing for the execution of, and successfully completing of the task. Someone always had to have the reins in their hands, even though the mules were gentle and knew where they were going. We knew that at any time an emergency could occur. A snake could suddenly appear out of the brush, the sound of a wildcat in the woods or a tractor in the next field could frighten the mules and they could start to run out of control. That is why we must always keep the Word in our hearts, and someone must always keep their hands on the reins of our ministry development.

Bitting allows the most blessed of us to submit to leadership correction and advice.

The bitting process is never over, no matter how high we go or what level of ministry we achieve. As leaders, there should always be someone to whom we can turn to share our visions and check our decisions. Every leader should have a covering of some kind. It can be an individual leader, a reformation, or a council, but one should never stand alone on his or her understanding. The vision may be clear but the process of turning it into reality may need some advising. Bitting allows the most blessed of us to submit to leadership correction and advice. If the teacher refuses teaching, that teacher has an unteachable spirit, a self-centered personality, and is egotistic. In a sense he or she is unbridled and may say something that would hurt the congregation.

As we develop as a Christian and move from one level of ministry to another with more responsibility as a leader, it is important to be aware of the factors that hinder spiritual growth. This will put us in a better position to overcome obstacles that are designed to hinder our growth and development as a leader. Our readiness as believers, and our growth and development as leaders is a part of God's plan for the church whether we are called to be an Apostle, Pastor, Teacher or any of the fivefold ministries, God wants a church that will not be defeated by the weapons of Satan's warfare against it. He desires that every believer grow in the grace and knowledge of God that will lead other men and women to Him.

Look at the parable of the talents in Matthew 25. Here we find God illustrating the need for spiritual growth and development. He is looking for believers, such as you and I, who are willing to faithfully use the giftedness that He has given us so that He can supply us with the spiritual increase we need to get the job done. If we can identify the barriers to our spiritual growth and development, and effectively deal with them, the church and its leadership as a whole can be productive in developing godly inspired commitments that will turn visions into reality. We must focus on the development of our Christian character that will make us living epistles and demonstrate the faithfulness that adds to the church daily and create an atmosphere of Holiness.

Spiritual immature leaders are a hindrance to both the believer and those who are connected to them. Hebrews 5:11-14 gives a clear picture of what Paul is saying; the NIV version makes it much clearer.

> *We have much to say about this, but it is hard to explain because you are slow to learn. In fact, though by this time you ought to be teachers, you need someone to teach you the elementary truths of God's word all over again. You need milk, not solid food! Anyone who lives on milk, being still an infant, is not acquainted with the teaching about righteousness. But solid food is for the mature, who by constant use have trained themselves to distinguish good from evil.*

Paul was concerned that the church at Corinth was immature and unable to receive solid food and still required a milk diet. It is obvious that the problem was that the saints were on milk because the leaders of the church were immature. They had assignments to teach, but could not because they, themselves, were babies and still unable to eat the solid food of the Word. Paul said it is understandable that the natural man or carnal men have a problem with discerning the spiritual things of God. Perhaps their carnality caused them to lean to their own understanding, do what was convenient for them, and to compromise the fundamental principles of righteousness whenever faced with a challenge.

> *And I, brethren, could not speak unto you as unto spiritual, but as unto carnal, even as unto babes in Christ. I have fed you with milk, and not with meat: for hitherto ye were not able to bear it, neither yet now are ye able. For ye are yet carnal: for whereas there is among you envying, and strife, and divisions, are ye not carnal, and walk as men?*
> *Corinthians 3:1-3*

Paul continues his ministry about the immature by focusing on the church at Colossi where he expresses his concern for those believers who focused on philosophy and the tradition of men fueled by the desire to satisfy the rudiment of the flesh as a worthy substitute for following Christ. Jesus commended Peter for his spiritual insight and revealed the true nature of his spiritual perception. Jesus said that Peter's understanding of who He was, was not revealed by flesh and blood, but by the heavenly Father. The church needs believers who will submit to the will of God in such a way that they are able to receive divinely inspired revelations.

Having a baby in one's home is a healthy sign of family growth. Though the baby requires much care and attention, he edifies the family and home. In the same sense, new believers in a church are not a problem but a welcome sign of increase. However, when these babes in Christ do not grow and mature over time, there is cause for concern.

> *Wherefore laying aside all malice, and all guile, and hypocrisies, and envies, and all evil speakings, as newborn babes, desire the sincere milk of the word, that ye may grow thereby:*
> *Peter 2:1-2*

There should be a process of bridling and bitting and sheltering from erroneous teachings.

As leaders, especially Pastors, we are to be most concerned about new converts: we must prepare for the nourishment in our preaching and teaching that will enable the believer to grow spiritually. We must organize new membership classes that are designed to give a good foundation upon which they can build good Christian character and develop integrity as believers. There should be a process of bridling and bitting and sheltering from erroneous teachings. There are too many premature deaths in Pentecost and malnourished believers due to a lack of commitment to training; too many self-inspired, self-taught unbridled ministers entering the priesthood with no covering. Babes and novices need covering. Salvation is too important to be placed into the hands of a novice.

CHAPTER THREE

THE WALL OF RESISTANCE
[Word Aflame, Expository series March 2003]

There has always been and perhaps will always be resistance to our efforts to move forward as believers in the Lord's church. Challenges will come from without and within. Perhaps we will be the biggest hindrance to our move from one level of ministry to the next will. Satan creates walls that are designed to dissuade us through discouragement, sometimes from our closest friends, family members, and or associates. The saddest thing about developing a character that will propel us to the next level is the resistance that comes from believers within the body of Christ. Nevertheless, we must remain steadfast, unmovable, and always abounding in the work of the Lord.

We must learn to trust God no matter what, and to follow the advice of Job, *"Though He slay me, yet will I trust Him."*

Leaning to one's own understanding and allowing the physical to determine our destiny is a hindrance to our growth and development as leaders in the Lord's Church. Fleshly dispositions also prohibit and limits spiritual growth. Envy, strife, divisions, and walking in the flesh all play their part in how much we mature as a leader. The opposite of envy is love; love does not rejoice in evil, but it rejoices in truth. When we feel out of character or upset when we hear of someone else's success or favor, we are experiencing the influence of "the spirit of envy." Envy is another form of jealousy. The baptized believer should at all cost avoid this spirit.

> *If we live in the Spirit, let us also walk in the Spirit. Let us not be desirous of vain glory, provoking one another, envying one another.*
> Galatians 5:25-26

If we consider jealousy to be the seedbed of a host of other acts of unrighteousness that comes out of a carnal heart, then we can understand how strife fits into this quartet of abominations mentioned in the Book of Proverbs. Strife is the mother of contention that comes out of resentment because of the elevation of someone you feel undeserving of it or for an equal being promoted over you. In Corinth we find Paul warning the Corinthians about being contentious toward their fellow labors in the church. Jude 3 tells us that believers should only *"earnestly contend for the faith that was once delivered unto the saints,"* and not against one another. Contention against one another is caused by strife that produces divisiveness. Paul exhorted the church to speak the same thing, to have the same mind, and the same judgment rather than to allow division to develop among them. There should be one voice, one vision, and one church. Paul demonstrated the destructiveness of division and utilized it in his defense before the Sanhedrin in Acts 23. He observed that the crowd opposed to his preaching was comprised of both Pharisees and Sadducees. He immediately identified himself with Pharisees and raised the question of the Resurrection, which was a point of great dissent between the two groups. Division and dissension resulted among the people so much so that the Sadducees desired to kill Paul, but thanks be to God, the chief captain rescued Paul from the melee because he sided with Paul's teaching of the resurrection.

Proverbs 6:19 lists seven things that are an abomination to God. One of these abominations is *"he that soweth discord among brethren."* Sowing discord and disharmony between fellow Christians is abominable to God, and Christians should avoid participating in such divisions.

> *These six things doth the LORD hate: yea, seven are an abomination unto him: A proud look, a lying tongue, and hands that shed innocent blood, an heart that deviseth wicked imaginations, feet that be swift in running to mischief, a false witness that speaketh lies, and he that soweth discord among brethren.*
> *Proverbs 6:16-19*

Walking after fleshly desires is another abomination that limits spiritual growth. Because the Corinthians displayed the spirits of envy, strife, division and fleshly inclinations, Paul declared that they were carnal and walked as men, or after the flesh. At least twice in his epistle to the Christians at Rome, Paul directed the believers to *"walk not after the flesh, but after the spirit."* (Romans 8:1) There is no condemnation to those engaged in a spiritual walk with Jesus Christ. Following the leading of the Holy Spirit keeps one from fulfilling the fleshly lusts of the carnal nature. (Galatians 5:16) Paul emphatically states, *"No flesh should glory in his presence."* (I Corinthians 1:29) I am led to the first Psalm of David.

> *Blessed is the man that walketh not in the counsel of the ungodly, nor standeth in the way of sinners, nor sitteth in the seat of the scornful. But his delight is in the law of the LORD; and in his law doth he meditate day and night. And he shall be like a tree planted by the rivers of water, that bringeth forth his fruit in his season; his leaf also shall not wither; and whatsoever he doeth shall prosper. The ungodly are not so: but are like the chaff which the wind driveth away. Therefore, the ungodly shall not stand in the judgment, nor sinners in the congregation of the righteous. For the LORD knoweth the way of the righteous: but the way of the ungodly shall perish.*
> *Psalm 1:1-6*

The carnal man by nature gravitates toward the physical: how it looks, how it feels, how it sounds, and the like. It is the seedbed for prejudicial preferences. Our prejudices cause us to place the power of who could or should be saved in our hands. It puts us in the same boat as Jonah when he allowed his feelings to get in the way of his assignment to go to Nineveh. On the Day of Pentecost Peter quoted the prophet Joel, *"It shall come to pass in the last days, saith God, I will pour out of my Spirit upon all flesh..."* (Acts 2:17) Just because we are saved and carry the title of Doctor, Reverend, Elder, Etc., this does not mean that we fully understand our responsibility as witnesses of Jesus, the Christ. Peter held fast to his Jewish convictions: eating only those things which were considered clean according to the Law, and dealing only with Jews when it came to God's promises. It wasn't until his vision in Acts 10 and his commission to go to Cornelius's house that his prejudice spirit was arrested. Like Peter, there were other Jews who felt that eating or associating with Gentiles was an abomination before God, but when Peter ministered to them and shared with them his vision, they too, ridded themselves of their prejudices against the Gentiles.

"Lean not to your own understanding." We as individuals in the Lord's church and baptized believers may never know who is worthy of becoming a follower of the lamb. If we look at the makeup of the church at Corinth, we will find that it did not have many who were wise or influential or even noble; instead, God chose the foolish, weak, lowly, and despised. We have been called and set apart as leaders in the church of God. We are to be living epistles and lights that lead men to the safety of God's will. It is not up to us as individuals to decide who we minister to, but to go where He leads us, say what He tells us, and whosoever will, let them come. It is important that we never forget the work of salvation and redemption God performed in our lives as arched as we were; if He could save us, He can save even the worse of sinners. Remember the words of Isaiah, *"Hearken to me, ye that follow after righteousness, ye that seek the Lord: look unto the rock whence ye are hewn, and to the hole of the pit whence ye are digged."* (Isaiah 51:1) We must not forget the lifestyle of sin from which we were saved, lest we return to it. The chosen have no choice; we must preach the Word in season and out of season.

Satan creates walls of separation within ministries and between individual in ministries. To break down these walls of division one must start with the sanctification of one's self by praying without ceasing, and commitment to the study of God's Word. Much has been written about the fruit of the flesh and how it can hinder the believer from maturing as a Christian. If we focus on the fruit of the Spirit, we can overcome the temptations that are associated with the fruit of the flesh. Loving God whom we have never seen should make it easy to love our neighbors who we see everyday. These are the words of Jesus to the church. Love is first mentioned in the fruit and seems to be the foundation of our Christian character; if you can love, you can empathize with failures of other; love hides a multitude of faults.

> *And above all things have fervent charity among yourselves: for charity shall cover the multitude of sins.*
> *1 Peter 4:8*

The love that we, as Christian, must have for our sisters and brothers must be fervent which means earnest, affectionate and sincere. Peter said that this love must be "above all things fervent," strong and lasting. It is greater than faith or hope, longsuffering or meekness.

> *Put on therefore, as the elect of God, holy and beloved, bowels of mercies, kindness, humbleness of mind, meekness, longsuffering; forbearing one another, and forgiving one another, if any man have a quarrel against any: even as Christ forgave you, so also do ye. And above all these things put on charity, which is the bond of perfectness.*
> *Colossians 3:12-14*

To cover or conceal the sins of others does not mean to justify; it simply means not to aggravate them or spread them among the brethren.

Peter also infers that Christians ought to have greater love toward each other than toward other men. I don't believe Peter here is referring to agonistic, adulterous, or men of apostate minds. Peter says that love is the foundation of forgiveness and patience, *"forbearing one another in love." "Let brotherly love continue,"* it is not enough to forgive one another or to bear each other's malice or even to show respect for each other. We must intensely and fervently love each other. Love is like the honey that the bee makes. We can't duplicate it or manufacture it; it must be genuine. True love is so divinely complex that its properties are so divinely ordained that it covers a multitude of sins. It inclines us to not only forgive but to also forget. To cover or conceal the sins of others does not mean to justify; it simply means not to aggravate them or spread them among the brethren. Love teaches us to love those who are weak and have been overtaken with a fault or who may have been guilty of an offence before they were saved.

Paul intimates that the whole law is fulfilled in one word, *"thou shalt love thy neighbor as thyself."* Paul here is concerned with our attitude and behavior towards each other and seeks to persuade us to let our love be evidenced of our sincere walk with God and as an instrument used to root out dissensions and divisions among us.

Other walls created by Satan are the lack of joy, peace, and longsuffering. Though these and other parts of the fruit of the Spirit have their own interpretations, let me first say that the fruit of the Spirit is an allegory for the renewed nature of man.

The joy of the Lord makes reference to the believer's constant delight in God. The peace referred to is our conscience or mindset or temperament or behavior towards others. Longsuffering deals with our patience to defer anger and our contentedness to bear injuries. Gentleness refers to having a sweetness of temper, especially towards those who encouraged us when others have wronged us. Goodness (kindness), faith, fidelity, justice, and honesty in what we profess and promise to others. Meekness wherewith to govern our passions and resentments so as not to be easily provoked, and temperance in meat and drink and other enjoyments of life, so as not to be excessive and immoderate in the use of them.
(From Matthew Henry's Commentary on the Whole Bible: New Modern Edition, Electronic Database. Copyright © 1991 by Hendrickson Publishers, Inc.)

There are other walls that affect our growth and development as true worshipers of Christ such as not understanding protocol, displaying unethical behavior and immaturity. Protocol deals with polity, being aware of the proper procedure at the proper time. Decorum covers a wide area of physical and intellectual behaviors: dignity and modesty.

Bitting Prevents Betrayal

As believers, we are so often unaware of the potential that lies within us. The potential, both to do good and to do evil is ever present. We often find it difficult to turn the light inward and see the areas in our own lives that need spiritual attention. Think for a moment of the times you found yourself in a dangerous and compromising situation and felt that you had gone too far to turn things around.

We need only to look at Judas Iscariot to discover our own potential to yield to the temptation of the enemy. We feel that we would never sink to the depths of betraying Jesus. Now we need to recognize the flaws that were in Judas and learn from them. For that same spirit and attitude can very stealthily take root in our own lives.

The development of our Christian character depends on our relationship with Jesus Christ. We must examine some important areas in our lives that we must regard if we are to avoid the terrible pit into which Judas fell. As believers and members of a local church or a part of a reformation, we are exposed to the same teaching, we are exposed to the same anointing, and we know well the vision of our leaders. If we yield to the rudiments of the flesh we would have little trouble derailing the visionary purpose God has given them. Although we are in prayer every prayer meeting night and are witness to the many miracles that occurred in the congregation, we must be mindful to the stealth of the enemy.

Judas must have been gifted and a man of some business astuteness to have been appointed as treasurer for the disciples and Jesus. The disciples depended on the resources of others to sustain them. Your giftedness may have placed you in a vital position in the vision of your leader. Therefore, you have to be watchful that Satan doesn't use your position and giftedness to inflate your ego and influence you to *"think of yourself to be more than you ought to think"* or to deceive you to believe that you can fulfill the vision that the Lord gave your leader better and faster than he or she can. We need not look for Satan to force himself into our hearts or to openly push himself into our decision making process. He stealthily or cautiously in a quiet manner plants the seed of rebellion and egotism in our hearts and waits for the opportue moment to act. He takes you to a place in your thinking where you should not be or don't want to be.

There is something prophetic about where Judas' name appeared in the listing of the disciples, he was always listed last. Prophetic or not, Judas was a member of the most select of Jesus which speaks volumes for you, the believer to recognize. Your position does not preclude you from being used by the enemy to work against the leadership of your ministry. Satan waits for an occasion to enter our hearts; therefore, we must keep ourselves steadfast, unmovable, and always abounding in the work of the Lord.

We do not know where Judas fell short in his commitment to Jesus but John tell us that Satan waited; he knew the content of Judas' character and that he had somewhere come short. Luke tells us of a woman who lost a coin; Matthew tells us of 5 virgins whose oil ran out. The Bible devotes a lot of time to exposing the lost. In each case the lost only discovered their weakness long after the anointing had left them. *"Samson shook himself; for he knew not that the spirit had left him."*

We must always pray – always. Satan waits for an opportunity to enter into our heart. Perhaps Judas at certain stages in his relationship with Jesus thought he was in a good place. When was the last time you turned the light inwardly on yourself, what are the weaknesses in your character that you found and still have not arrested? John says that Judas was always a thief; even though he experienced all the wonders and miracles that the other disciples experienced, he failed to surrender to the Spirit of the Lord.

Those who walk away from ministry after they have openly and publicly committed to its support have in a sense betrayed the trust that their leader put in them. Even though the pastor or other leaders in the ministry do not physically show it, they are hurt. A father or a mother always feels the pain of losing a child. Judas betrayed Jesus with a kiss. The pain of that kiss was far more severe and intensely painful to Jesus than the soldiers scourging with the whip or their piercing of His side with the sword. David in Psalm 55 expressed the emotional pain of being betrayed by a friend.

> *For it was not an enemy that borne it: neither was it he that hated me that did magnify himself against me; then I would have hid myself from him: but it was thou, a man mine equal, my guide, and mine acquaintance.*
> *Psalm 55:12-13*

The gravity of your betrayal of your leader's trust goes far beyond the act of leaving a ministry.

Not only does your leader put trust in you, but also others in the ministry have connected to you as a believer because of your leader's trust in you. You may not only have affected the trust of your leader and the progress of his vision, but you may have affected the lives of other believers within the ministry who trusted your anointing and connected themselves to you because of it. The gravity of your betrayal of your leader's trust goes far beyond the act of leaving a ministry. We must always be mindful that our salvation is bigger than we are; it is bigger than our pride and our feelings. Our image of ourselves must take a back seat to our responsibility as Christians. In spite of your betrayal your leader must still treat you as if you had done nothing. After Jesus knew that Judas had betrayed Him, after Judas had kissed Him, after He knew that the soldiers were waiting for the signal to apprehend Him, He called Judas "friend" and said, "Why have you come here?" Isaiah describes the deep inner pain of Jesus as *"stricken, smitten, and afflicted, a man of sorrows, and acquainted with grief."*

History is replete with individuals who have betrayed their trust, their cause, or their friends. Perhaps no word in any language is more repulsive or carries more revulsion than that of "traitor." Like Judas, the betrayal of your leader's trust is more likely to be short lived or for temporary pleasure. The betrayal of your trust is, in comparison, selling out to appease the pride you had hidden in your heart. It was worse than Esau selling his birthright for a bowl of soup. At lease Judas' conscience weighed upon him, but to no avail. Peter's denial of Jesus was no less bad as Judas' betrayal, but Peter faced Jesus with his guilt while Judas choose to hang himself.

> *The Son of man goeth as it is written of him: but woe unto that man by whom the Son of man is betrayed! It had been good for that man if he had not been born.*
> Matthew 26:24

These things are written for our learning; Solomon taught us to incline our ear unto wisdom, and apply our heart to understanding. (Proverbs 2:2) We must learn from the lives, successes, and mistakes of others. The sad commentary of the life of Judas can teach us some valuable lessons and warn us of some pending pitfalls. Those who make vows to support pastoral visions and then break those vows are in comparison to Judas' betrayal of Jesus, and in fact crucify to themselves their leaders afresh and put them to an open shame. How tragic that the steward subverts the vision of the visionary. Paul wrote in Romans 12:9 *"Let your love be sincere"* (let it be real). We bring shame to our leaders when our commitment is fickle, when we are easily steered away from the things that reinforce the visionary purpose of the pastor or other leaders. He admonished us to *"be no more children, tossed to and fro, and carried about with every wind of doctrine, by the sleight of men, and cunning craftiness, whereby they lie in wait to deceive."* (Ephesians 4:14)

There is always a spirit of compromise tugging at God's people. The world tries continually to lure Christians away from real commitment and devotion to their leaders as well as the church. The god of this world is Satan, and he wants others to fall with him. It is no use ignoring the tug of the world. The only way we can defeat the tricks of the enemy is by actively resisting the temptation he lays before us. Serving God involves more than speaking in tongues, being baptized, paying tithes, and using our gifts to exhort the Lord. We must pay our vows, keep our word, and live according to our testimonies. If we find fault with our fellow laborers, go to them. Be living epistles, steadfast, unmovable, and always abounding in the work of the Lord. If we return back to the things from which God has delivered us we make ourselves transgressors.
(Galatians 2:18)

> ***Un-harnessed ambitions lead to prideful spirits that are, in most cases, un-teachable, and egotistic.***

Man's impatience has led him on a declining path. God often has great and precious things in store for us, but because we are unwilling to wait for them we often lose them. Un-harnessed ambitions lead to prideful spirits that are, in most cases, un-teachable, and egotistic. It leads to carnality and the grabbing for things to fulfill lustful desires and in most cases the loss of everything as well as disgrace and shame.

CHAPTER FOUR

SEEDS THAT BITTING PRODUCE

This gospel is not ours; we are merely servants of the Most High; we serve according to our several abilities. One man plants, another waters, and God gives the increase. Among the gifts God gave to the church, the ministry of preaching and teaching are of the most important. The five-fold ministry mentioned in Ephesians 4:11 is for the perfection of the church. If this Gospel be hidden, it is hidden to those that are lost. In the Parable of the Sower in Matthew 13, Jesus taught that the seed was the Word of God. The seed of God's Word can be very productive if it is planted in the right soil. The Word of God must be sown to be of any effect as a witness of God's saving power.

Who knows the power of a seed? Who knows the power of the Word of God? We can count the number of seeds in an apple, but who knows the number of apples in a seed. Seeds will hold their substance until planted or placed in a place where they can germinate. It is important that we chose good ground in which to sow. Paul admonished us to turn over the fallow ground that is to prepare it for sowing. We must understand and trust that the environment in which we sow to produce our harvest has to be properly prepared. Some plants can't survive in certain environments. The seed may germinate and the plant spout, but if the climate and the environment is not conducive to the plant it will not produce a harvest.

One does not sow a seed and forget about it. After the planting of the seed, which is the gospel, it is necessary to nurture, care for, and cultivate the ground around the plant until harvest. This may require a bitting process. As recorded in Acts18, Paul arrived in Corinth and ministered there for one and one-half years sowing the gospel. It was not an easy task; his ministry faced many challenges. He had been beaten, cast into jail, and threaten for his life, but Paul had God's assurance that his ministry was necessary and that he was not to be afraid. Because you have been chosen as a sower or have been blessed with giftedness does not mean that you have "arrived." Too often those who are gifted are selective in their sowing. They use their gifts for personal gain and not for the benefit of furthering the Gospel.

The Preacher in Ecclesiastes tells us that there is a time and a season for planting and for reaping. The seed (wisdom) gained through bitting will produce rewarding results, but remember that we still face enemies who dare to sow tares in our fields of opportunities. Amid our trust in God and our obedience to His will for our lives, we must prepare for unexpected challenges and disappointments, but the bitting process teaches us to endure hardness as good soldiers and to seize the favorable opportunities for every good purpose and work. There is always something to do in ministry; none were called to a visionary purpose to sit idle.

The writer of Ecclesiastes 3 also said there is a time to "rend," to tear apart, to split. Amid challenge and disappointment there is a time for mourning and sorrow, but keep in mind that one cannot mourn forever. There is always a set time for mourning then the season of repair begins. We must trust that all things work together for the good of those who are called according to His purpose.

Bitting produces good leaders, but before one can become a good leader he or she must first have been a good follower. Good stewardship fosters good leadership. When one is able to take care of another man's possessions, he in turn will enjoy the favor of others taking care of his possessions when he is elevated to leadership. Good stewards do not envy their master's favor, but under girds it and guards it from those who would sow tares or discord to divert the vision's purpose

Integrity is another reward of good stewardship. It takes integrity to give ownership to the visionary when in fact it was you who did most of the groundwork to bring the vision to reality. One of the tricks of the enemy is to get you to murmur and complain because you are not credited for the success of another man's vision when you did most of the work. Deborah did not seek ownership of the victory of Israel over Sisera and Jabin's army when in fact it was her inspiration that lead Barak to victory.

Astuteness is the product of developing good study habits and listening skills. Before one can be any kind of spiritual leader, he or she must develop a good biblical foundation:

Bible history, hermeneutics, and exegeses of its contents. One must listen to fortify his faith and commitment to vision and purpose. Listening helps one to avoid many of the pitfalls that accompany visionary purpose. Listening is a ministry in and of itself. Studying plants seeds of the gospel in the heart of the believer. It is the Word that keeps us from sinning against the commandments of God. David said, *"Thou Word have I hid in my heart."* Without the Word of God, it is impossible to commit to visionary purpose because purpose always suffers challenge from without and sometime from within. It is our affirmations of faith that keeps us grounded on the promises of God. We must study to show ourselves approved, ready, and worthy of God's divine interaction.

Spiritual Bitting Assessment Results

Servant leaders have an increased awareness of strengths, competencies and attitudes. They have an understanding and knowledge of the key components needed to effect positive change. Servant leaders have increased effectiveness and endurance levels; they are able to better affect team performance, encourage focus and direction for team members dealing with change and challenges. They have faithfully served as obedient followers. Spiritual as well as natural growth is evident in their critical thinking processes.

> *God uses leaders who will endure hardness, stay right where they are and fight the good fight of faith until Satan is conquered.*

Spiritual bitting enables one to harness the strength required to endure hardness as a good soldier. God uses leaders who will endure hardness, stay right where they are and fight the good fight of faith until Satan is conquered. Rick Renner, Author of

"Living in the Combat Zone" warns about developing notions of drifting (not being able to stay in one place long enough to do anything for God). "When God calls you to do something, and it is hard, your mind may drift to other things. If you aren't truly committed to what God told you to do right where you are, you may be tempted to think your drifting mind is the leading of the Holy Spirit. It is difficult to "endure hardness." The devil hates what you are attempting to do in your city, your ministry, your business, your church, or your family. He can't bear the thought of God winning another fight!" (Rick Renner)

> *He who tills his land will have plenty of bread, But he who follows frivolity will have poverty enough!*
> *Proverbs 28:19*

SECTION TWO

CHAPTER FIVE

CHRIST'S SECOND COMING

As believers who have perfected our faith in Christ Jesus through the bitting process that leads to the development of our Christian character, one of our concerns should be pure and Holy living by believing in whom we worship as we await the arrival of the soon coming King. Jesus is soon to come and it would be remiss of me to not recognize this fact. In spite of the doubt of some unbelievers, Paul's letters to the Thessalonians makes more than 20 references to the fact that Jesus will return. This is the Hope of the Church. Let me assure you that Paul ended every chapter of his first letter to the Thessalonians with the assurance that the Lord will return. *"And to wait for his Son from heaven, whom he raised from the dead, even Jesus, which delivered us from the wrath to come."*

> *For what is our hope, or joy, or crown of rejoicing? Are not even ye in the presence of our Lord Jesus Christ at his coming? For ye are our glory and joy.*
> *1 Thessalonians 2:19-20*

> *To the end he may stablish your hearts unblameable in holiness before God, even our Father, at the coming of our Lord Jesus Christ with all his saints.*
> *1 Thessalonians 3:13*

> *Then we which are alive and remain shall be caught up together with them in the clouds, to meet the Lord in the air: and so shall we ever be with the Lord. Wherefore comfort one another with these words.*
> *1 Thessalonians 4:17-18*

> *And the very God of peace sanctify you wholly; and I pray God your whole spirit and soul and body be preserved blameless unto the coming of our Lord Jesus Christ.*
> *1 Thessalonians 5:23*

The first coming of the Lord was sudden and a surprise to the philosophers of His time, but there will be no mistake of who He is at His seconding coming for Paul tells the Thessalonians that He will appear with the shout of an archangel.

> *For the Lord himself shall descend from heaven with a shout, with the voice of the archangel, and with the trump of God: and the dead in Christ shall rise first:*
> *1 Thessalonians 4:16*

Paul was not alone on this missionary journey; Timothy and Silas were with him. When Paul went to Corinth he sent this letter to the Thessalonians by Timothy. However, when Timothy arrived in Thessalonica he found that there were concerns among the people about the second coming of Christ.

They were worried about their loved ones who had gone on before them. Will they see them again, will they know them? False teachers had propagated erroneous doctrines about the second coming of Christ that affected the attitude of the people, especially the new converts.

As leaders in the Lord's Church, we should be concerned when we hear of, so called, preachers, prophets, and even pastors, who abuse their trust by taking advantage of the membership. The Church is overly inundated with unethically elevated, so called leaders whose only purpose for preaching is either to fulfill personal desires and ambitions, or to teach based on their own private interpretation and erroneous doctrines.

The believer must remain righteous and sober, "looking for that blessed hope."

Paul's love for the church at Thessalonica prompted him to address these issues in his first letter. He was concerned about the teaching that had affected the new converts and the belief of the church about the second coming of Christ. Paul's letter becomes very intimate. He uses the term "Brothers and Sisters," more than a dozen times in his writings. He continues in his writing in Titus to say that we should have no doubt about Christ's return; He is coming. The believer must remain righteous and sober, "looking for that blessed hope."

> *Teaching us that, denying ungodliness and worldly lusts, we should live soberly, righteously, and godly, in this present world; Looking for that blessed hope, and the glorious appearing of the great God and our Saviour Jesus Christ;*
> *Titus 2:12-13*

As stewards of God, we must only do that which pleases God; don't try to flatter God. Do what God has called you to do for the glory of God, and always seek to encourage God's people. As leaders we should always be prayerful. Paul encouraged the church by saying; "We give thanks to God always for you all, making mention of you in our prayers." One of the things I always advise new leaders who are developing new ministries is to develop a list of perspective member from people you meet; pray for them and keep in touch with them. One of the weaknesses of new ministries is follow-up with new converts.

There are some things that Jesus, the Son of God, did not know because He was incarnated in the flesh.

In all that we know about what Paul taught concerning the second coming of Christ, he never said when it would occur, yet there are those who say that they know when it will be. The Bible emphatically states that not even Jesus knows the day or time God will return. Let me say something about the "Doctrine of Incarnation," because of it, even Jesus confessed that He did not know the time of the end. This may be difficult to accept, but it demonstrates the geniuses and completeness of His humanity. When God added humanity to His previously unmitigated deity, He willingly embraced the limitation of that existence; including boundaries of the knowledge of the Son of God. This is beyond our comprehension, but we accept it as a miraculous consequence of the manifestation of God in the flesh. There are some things that Jesus, the Son of God, did not know because He was incarnated in the flesh. Only the God in Him was Omniscient.

Although we cannot know the day and the time when the Lord will return, some say we can know the season, but Jesus said that we cannot know even the season. Paul said in 1 Thessalonians 5:1-2, *"But of the times and the seasons, brethren, ye have no need that I write unto you. For yourselves know perfectly that the day of the Lord so cometh as a thief in the night."* Jesus' teaching about the end-times was so rooted in the mind of His disciples that they saw no need to discuss it. Paul thought that it was so near that it could occur during his life time; he wrote:

> *For this we say unto you by the word of the Lord, that we, which are alive and remain unto the coming of the Lord shall not prevent them which are asleep. For the Lord himself shall descend from heaven with a shout, with the voice of the archangel, and with the trump of God: and the dead in Christ shall rise first: Then we which are alive and remain shall be caught up together with them in the clouds, to meet the Lord in the air: and so shall we ever be with the Lord.*
> *1 Thessalonians 4:15-17*

Only the God, in the Christ, is omniscient.

In this generation the believer should live in expectation of Christ's return, and not waste time in fruitless speculation; preaching that Jesus knows all things may be a misunderstanding or a misinterpretation of the scripture. Only the God, in the Christ, is omniscient.

Our ministries should be seasoned with care; we should have servant's hearts. We should preach not to please man but to please God. We should seek to convince new converts to serve God with all their hearts, soul and mind. We must not seek to be wealthy from our preaching, but care for the flock of God as a father cares for his children; gently nursing them to a healthy lifestyle as a baptized believer in the Lord's Church.

There are too many in the body of Christ who are not walking a straight and narrow path; they are "marrying and giving in to marriage." That is to say, in every age there have been men of corrupt minds that have endeavored to subvert the fundamental principles of the Gospel. As there are preachers now, who call themselves true prophets, but are really not, so were there Sadducees in our Savior's time, that bantered the doctrine of the resurrection of the dead, though they were plainly revealed in the Old Testament, and were articles of the Jewish faith. The Sadducees deny that there is any resurrection.

The church is a vehicle of faith and goes through seasons of struggle and reward. Pastors don't always share the love that the congregation has for them. They are inundated with both social and economic pressures as well as spiritual weaknesses from without and from within. It is always rewarding for a leader to learn that the congregation cherishes his or her leadership. The old saying, "everything that shines is not gold," is a true one. No one knows what leaders have to go through to portray a successful image, and what sometimes is or appears to be spiritually a success, may at the same time be an economic disaster.

Paul gleaned from stronger churches to help the weaker ones; his labor in the work of the ministry was not for his own prosperity. Paul made it clear to the churches he visited that he did not come to be a burden on the ministry:

> *Neither did we eat any man's bread for nought; but wrought with labour and travail night and day, that we might not be chargeable to any of you: Not because we have not power, but to make ourselves an ensample unto you to follow us.*
> *2 Thessalonians 3:8-9*

As we await the second coming of Christ, we should not sit idly waiting for His glorious appearing.

He expressed the joy he felt when Timothy brought him a good report from Thessalonica. He also spoke of how much they longed for him to come and of their expectation to hear him speak to them of God's love for them. Paul's concern for the church was that every believer be encouraged to live righteous, be consistent in his walk with God, live a pure and set apart life, and love one another. As we await the second coming of Christ, we should not sit idly waiting for His glorious appearing.

CHAPTER SIX

BARRIERS TO RESPONSIBILITY

Barriers to the continuation of a strong church may lie in the level of spiritual astuteness the member of the current church leaders received from the church leaders who were before them. This too requires a sort of bitting or teaching or grounding. We not only have a responsibility to be living epistles, we also bear the responsibility of passing on what God has blessed us to know of His love and kindness to the next generation of believers. I always compared this Christian walk to a marathon race, where the runner must successfully complete several athletic challenges to win the race. However, there is another race that is a part of the track and field event that best allegorizes the responsibilities of church leaders in today's church. It is the relay race where the most important responsibility of the runner is the passing of the baton to the next runner of the race. We have for so long placed much emphases on running the race, living righteously, being steadfast and unmovable, and abounding in the work of the Lord, but Paul in his letter to Timothy, reminds us that, we not only have a responsibility to live right but to pass on to our children and children's children, to the next generation of believers the love, faith, and principle of godliness that will make them as true believers standing on a firm foundation.

Moses admonished the people to always remember where they were, and not to forget that He, the Lord, brought them out of the bondage of Egypt, out of the house of Pharaoh, from worshiping idle gods, and when they would not hear Moses, God called them to Mt. Horeb and spoke to them Himself.

> *And what nation is there so great, that hath statutes and judgments so righteous as all this law, which I set before you this day? Only take heed to thyself, and keep thy soul diligently, lest thou forget the things which thine eyes have seen, and lest they depart from thy heart all the days of thy life: but teach them thy sons, and thy sons' sons; specially the day that thou stoodest before the LORD thy God in Horeb, when the LORD said unto me, Gather me the people together, and I will make them hear my words, that they may learn to fear me all the days that they shall live upon the earth, and that they may teach their children.*
> *Deuteronomy 4:8-10*

Joshua and Caleb were the only two who escaped the bondage of Egypt in their generation, to enter the Promised Land, and this was because of their steadfast faith in God that set them apart from others in their generation. The children of the first generation that left Egypt and entered the Promised Land may have had some faith in God, but they failed to follow through in their faith by disobeying God. God had commanded them to drive out from the land that they had now inherited all of the Canaanites, which they failed to do. Their laxity and dabbling in the worship of Baal and Ashtaroth caused the next generation to grow up without any role models of faith, integrity, and love of the one true God.

Astaroth (also Ashtaroth, Astarot and Asteroth), in demonology, is the Great Duke of Hell, in the first hierarchy with Beelzebub and Lucifer; he is part of the evil trinity. He is a male figure named after the Mesopotamian goddess Ishtar.

They were too young to remember the remarkable deliverance from Egypt, the giving of the Law at Sinai, and the conquest of the Promised Land. Having no one to teach them about God set them to slowly drift away from God toward the worship of Baal and Ashtaroth. They intermarried with the nations around them and adopted their ungodly lifestyles.

Too often we do just enough in our worship and devotion to God to satisfy what we appear to be as believers or church members. We dress Holy, pay our tributes, attend our meetings, and learn our catechisms, but we never develop a personal relationship with God. We have become as the second generation of Jews that left Egypt who pledged to purge the land of idolatry and drive out the heathen inhabitants, but they failed to do so. Instead, they drove them out of just enough territory to establish a comfortable place for themselves to settled down in; they enjoyed their new possessions and grew familiar with their neighbors to the extent of entering into covenants with them. Instead of separating themselves from the inhabitance of the land, they gave their sons and daughters in marriage with the people of the land and succumbed to the lure of their foreign gods.

> *And an angel of the LORD came up from Gilgal to Bochim, and said, I made you to go up out of Egypt, and have brought you unto the land which I sware unto your fathers; and I said, I will never break my covenant with*

> *you. And ye shall make no league with the inhabitants of this land; ye shall throw down their altars: but ye have not obeyed my voice: why have ye done this? Wherefore I also said, I will not drive them out from before you; but they shall be as thorns in your sides, and their gods shall be a snare unto you.*
> Judges 2:1-3

Biblical astuteness is one of leadership's formidable weapons

It is important that we, as baptized believers, obey God and teach our children, both spiritually and biologically, who God is, what God is, and how to worship God in spirit and in truth. God expects us to teach and train our children the history of the Church, the principles and doctrines of Church, how to live a holy and set apart life for Christ. But how can the leaders of this generation's, New Testament church be instructors of truth if they themselves are lacking in the knowledge of the scripture. Biblical astuteness is one of leadership's formidable weapons in the quest to pass onto the next generation the oracles of God.

> *We will not hide them from their children, shewing to the generation to come the praises of the LORD, and his strength, and his wonderful works that he hath done. For he established a testimony in Jacob, and appointed a law in Israel, which he commanded our fathers, that they should make them known to their children: That the generation to come might know them, even the children which should be born; who should arise and declare them to their children: That they might set their hope in God, and not forget the works of God, but keep his commandments:*
> Psalm 78:4-7

Children are fast to notice what their parents do; they easily adopt what elders around them do, and are more easily to imitate the thinking and feelings of their peers. It behooves the leaders of today's church to believe and do what they say. They should strive to earn the confidence and respect of those over which they have oversight as well as the judgment and opinions of other leaders. When the congregation and subordinate leaders believe that their leader's astuteness is greater than their own, they feel they can rely implicitly on them.

> *When we fail to know what God requires, we hinder the growth and development of our congregations and the next generation of believers connected to us.*

As leaders and fathers in our own churches and reformations, we have a solemn responsibility to study the Word of God, to hermeneutically interpret the scripture, and with wisdom make it applicable in the lives of every believer connected to us as ministers of God. When we fail to know what God requires, we hinder the growth and development of our congregations and the next generation of believers connected to us.

Paul weights in on the importance of this responsibility by reminding Timothy of the role his mother and grandmother played in his own foundation of Godliness.

> *To Timothy, my dearly beloved son: Grace, mercy, and peace, from God the Father and Christ Jesus our Lord. I thank God, whom I serve from my forefathers with pure conscience, that without ceasing I have remembrance of thee in my prayers night and day; greatly desiring to see thee, being mindful of thy tears, that I may be filled with joy; When I call to remembrance the unfeigned faith that is in thee, which dwelt first in thy grandmother Lois, and thy mother Eunice; and I am persuaded that in thee also.*
> 2 Timothy 1:2-5

Lois, Eunice, and Timothy: three successive generations shared the same "unfeigned" faith. When Paul composed his letter to Timothy, he may have been comparing it to his own Jewish heritage and the faith he had received from his forefathers. Although Paul was now a baptized believer, he did not despise his Hebrew background. Paul met Timothy and his mother and, it is assumed, his grandmother in the new church that had been established in Lystra. Timothy's father was Greek, but Luke carefully pointed out that his mother was a Jewess who believed.

> *Then came he to Derbe and Lystra: and, behold, a certain disciple was there, named Timotheus, the son of a certain woman, which was a Jewess, and believed; but his father was a Greek:*
> Acts 16:1

Paul describes Timothy as having unfeigned faith. Faith that is sincere, wholehearted, and heartfelt. Unfeigned mean genuine in feeling, sincere, absence of hypocrisy, feigning, or any falsifying embellishment or exaggeration. In his letter Paul commended Timothy for being "wise unto salvation," for he was well schooled in the scriptures at a young age. He urged Timothy to continue in the unfeigned faith he had learned. It is important to note that Timothy could have chosen to follow the path of his father and become the student of philosophy, instead he chose a path of faith because of the teaching of his mother and grandmother.

World Aflame, March 2013 internalizing the message: The New Covenant community, like the Old, is confronted by choices. We can either be distracted, be conforming to the world around us, or we can commit to loving Jesus in covenant obedience. We have the same mandate as Israel to pass on our faith and heritage to the next generation. If we do not, we are violating our covenant vows.

Let us do everything in our power to pass the faith along to the next generation.

As grandparents and parents, leaders and overseers, we have no idea of the force and power of our example. No one lives to himself. We are always influencing those around us, either for good or for evil. Our children see our behaviors, and what they see us do, they assume it is right; therefore, they will imitate it. We must strive to be living epistles of Christ that our families and congregations can read. We can be examples of sincerity, genuineness, and truthfulness.

Very few Christian denominations keep their faith and fervor for more three generations. The truth and revival that many of them received in the eighteenth century have faded. But history does not have to repeat itself within the Pentecostal ranks. Let us do everything in our power to pass the faith along to the next generation.

CHAPTER SEVEN

OBEDIENCE

The bitting process requires that a believer have a submissive and obedient spirit. Most new converts have to be trained to be submissive to leadership. Their bridling and bitting must be tempered by teaching. It is during the initial birthing of the new believer when the leadership must minister to the "old man" to change its Adamic nature. This is done by feeding it milk.

> *Therefore, putting aside all malice and all deceit and hypocrisy and envy and all slander, like newborn babies,*

> *long for the pure milk of the word, so that by it you may grow in respect to salvation, if you have tasted the kindness of the Lord.*
> *1 Peter 2:1-2*

Peter in his first epistle, chapter 2, refers to the new convert as a "new born babe" who is, in some way, still responsive to the old man; the old man feeds on evil-speaking, malice and the guile that is in the heart; these characteristics of the flesh hinder us from profiting by the Word of God. A new life in Christ Jesus needs suitable food. Infants desire milk, it is easier for them to process. Our Lord, Jesus Christ, was merciful to us as sinners. As miserable as we were, we enjoyed the fullness of his Graces as we transitioned from one stage of grace to the other. New converts must through a process of obedience and submissiveness move from milk to meat. We only need as servants of God in this life to taste of the consolation of God to desire more of Him.

> ***Obedience is better than sacrifices and the most fervent prayers and the highest praises are not acceptable except through obedience to Jesus Christ.***

We must teach new believers that Christ is the Chief-Cornerstone and that He is their protection and security, the foundation on which they are built. He is precious in the excellence of His manifestation and solvent in His resolve. All true believers are a "holy priesthood," sacred to God, serviceable to others, endowed with heavenly gifts and graces. We must teach them that obedience is better than sacrifices and that the most fervent prayers and the highest praises are not acceptable except through obedience to Jesus Christ.

The lack of obedience leads to self-motivation and leaning to one's own understanding; one must acknowledge that a failure to acknowledge God is, in the least, selfish endeavors. Disobedience leads to thinking that what one is doing is for God's glory, when in fact; it is the product of vain ambition.

Babies in Christ react and respond to things according to the flesh; they are moved by their carnal self: how it taste or feels or looks or sounds. They must be taught to discern the moving of the spirit, to recognize the voice of God, and to try the spirit by the Word of God. They must be taught to study and the value of God's Word as it relates to the development of their Christian character. We must teach new converts that it is obedience that leads to promotion and elevation, not gifts. New converts must become a part of the fabric of the church; they must build their lives on the true foundation founded through the blood of Jesus. The believer must learn that Christ is the Chief Cornerstone that unites the whole congregation of believers into one everlasting body and that it is He who bears the weight of the whole fabric of the church. New converts must learn that they are chosen to stand on the foundation of the Church which is everlasting and precious beyond compare, then they will gravitate toward more obedience in Christ Jesus than toward making sacrifice.

How particular is God when it comes to Obedience? There is no greater example of obedience to God's word than is found in Genesis 6. God tells Noah to build the Ark; He gives Noah the instructions:

> *And this is the fashion which thou shalt make it of: The length of the ark shall be three hundred cubits, the breadth of it fifty cubits, and the height of it thirty cubits. A window shalt thou make to the ark, and in a cubit shalt thou finish it above; and the door of the ark shalt thou set in the side thereof; with lower, second, and third stories shalt thou make it. Genesis 6:15-16*

The twenty-second verse tells us that Noah obeyed God according to his commandments. God was well pleased with Noah because of His obedience to the Words of God. His obedience is a living testimony to the church today. Noah never deviated from what God instructed him to do; every board was cut and laid in place according to God's plan: the window, the door, and every level. The importance of obeying God cannot be over emphasized. Paul referenced it in this manner:

> *Wherefore, my beloved, as ye have always obeyed, not as in my presence only, but now much more in my absence, work out your own salvation with fear and trembling.*
> *Philippians 2:12*

One should not have to be watched or forced to obey God, directly or indirectly, by the leadership of them to whom He has given oversight.

We should aim to be as obedient to God's Will as Christ was

Keep in mind that you will never get out of sacrifice what you will get out of obedience. Consider what happened to Saul (I Samuel 15) because of his disobedience; he lost his kingdom and his favor with God. Jonah's refusal to obey God resulted in him being swallowed by a great fish and brought to where God purposed him to be. There is a price to pay for disobedience. I John 3:4 says, *"Whosoever committeth sin transgresseth also the law: for sin is the transgression of the law."* Because of Adam and Eve's sin we are called "the sons of disobedience," therefore we engage in a kind of spiritual warfare against our own natural tendency to disobey God. We should aim to be as obedient to God's Will as Christ was when He "became obedient to the point of death." (Phil 2:8)

God rejected His chosen people because of their disobedience to his will; they were lead into captivity for seventy years, they suffered under the hands of hard taskmasters: The Babylonians, the Medo-Persians, the Greeks, and finally the Romans. The most important thing to remember is that your failure to obey God does not put you completely out of His care; He is always just a prayer away. He cried out for Israel amid her folly, for her to return unto Him. He is always ready to receive you and heal your brokenness. Though your world has fallen around you and broke into a thousand pieces, Jesus, who is our sure foundation, is listening to hear your repentant cry; so without fear you have access to God through Jesus Christ our Lord.

Bitting bring us to a place in Christ where we will see it as a source of abundant blessing, a higher level of maturity, increased integrity and Christian character that will draw men unto Christ. As the Lord speaks to you, move without fear, no matter how crazy it looks. If He says jump through a wall, your responsibility is to jump, it is God's job to move the wall or make a hole in it.

Nothing infringes upon the authority of leadership more than the disobedience of its followers. The reality of visionary purpose is deeply embedded in the obedience of the believers over which God gave Pastors oversight. God gives the vision the to the leader or in the case of the Church, to Pastor. The fulfillment of his visionary purpose is centered on the attitude of the people. *"Where there is no vision the people perish."* However, where there is no commitment, dedication, or devotion or obedience (no people), the vision will also perish. Obedience is founded upon trust, dependability, and accountability. If your leader can count on you as an obedient follower, he or she will feel safe with you and trustworthy.

Obedience must be bonded with purity of intent.

All who attach themselves to leadership don't do it because of their belief in the purpose of the leader. Some use the ambitions of the leadership to fuel their own selfish desires; their fellowship is limited to how much the leader's popularity enhances their own ambition. Obedience must be bonded with purity of intent. There is no greater example of true fellowship and commitment to purpose than that of Ruth, *"Where you go, I will go; where you lodge, I will lodge; your God will be my God; where you are buried, I will be buried."* We see no ulterior motive in her resolve. She simply spoke out of the content of her heart.

> *For those things that proceeds out of the mouth comes from the heart... For out of the overflow of the heart, the mouth speaks.*
> *Mathews 12:34; 15:18*

Obedience is not something we are born with innately; it is an area of our character we learn through our suffering. (Hebrews 5:8) Our obedience to leadership increases as our faith increases and as our Christian character is developed.

> *Paul, a servant of Christ Jesus, called to be an apostle and set apart for the gospel of God— the gospel he promised beforehand through his prophets in the Holy Scriptures regarding his Son, who as to his earthly life was a descendant of David, and who through the Spirit of holiness was appointed the Son of God in power by his resurrection from the dead: Jesus Christ our Lord. Through him we received grace and apostleship to call all the Gentiles to the obedience that comes from faith for his name's sake. And you also are among those Gentiles who are called to belong to Jesus Christ.*
> *Romans 1:1-6*

There is this abstract perception of obedience that we hold dear to our hearts; it is ours to possess and to retain, to master through submissiveness, and to learn how to develop its effectiveness through faith. While using it as an instrument, we must take captive the knowledge of God that strengthens our Christian character. We must also take captive every thought of disobedience that is designed to destroy our unwavering faith in God and our obedience to Him through Jesus Christ.

Cheap grace means living without the demand of obedience upon us.

In *The Cost of Discipleship,* Dietrich Bonhoeffer penned the words; "Cheap grace is grace without discipleship, grace without the cross, grace without Jesus Christ, living and incarnate." Cheap grace means living as though God ignores or condones our sins. But forgiveness means that sin is real, and must be dealt with. We cannot ignore it, because God does not ignore it. The denial of sin is not grace: it is a lie. Cheap grace means living without the demand of obedience upon us.

In the book of Judges one of the recurring themes is, *"every man did that which was right in his own eyes."* When believers in our church are not held to a standard of obedience, the tone of our ministries become, "Do your own thing" and tolerance becomes the attitude of leadership. When no guidelines or principles are taught, nothing is out of order and thus nothing is looked upon as "sin," for without the law there is no sin. Nothing is clearly right or wrong, and thus, according to Dietrich Bonhoeffer, nothing can be labeled as "sinful," and thus there is no need to repent or ask for forgiveness. Jesus said, "If you love me you will keep my commandment." Keeping the commandments is to obey; furthermore, "all disobedience is sin and the wages of sin is death. John teaches us that God requires us to be obedient to His word and to commit to His will.

The bitting process helps in the development of the spirit of obedience; we have been taught that all disobedience is sin. Disobedience is caused by yielding to one's self-willingness to rebel against the authority of leadership. When God told Adam not to eat from the tree of the knowledge of good and evil He also told him of the consequence of his action, the consequence of disobedience. We must keep in mind that the Lord's word is never without effect. He said to Adam, "the day you eat, you will die." Although Adam did not immediately die physically, and went on to live for more than 800 years, he died spiritually that very minute; his very spirit was contaminated, and Adam entered into a state of spiritual death and passed it on to every descendent of the human race.

> *Therefore, as by one man, sin entered into the world and death by sin, so death passed onto all humans for all have sinned. Romans 5:12 KJV*

> *Therefore, just as sin entered the world through one man, and death through sin, and in this way death came to all people, because all sinned. Romans 5:12 NIV*

Although we, as individuals, did not personally disobey God by eating from the tree of knowledge, we are personally accountable for our own sinful acts of disobedience. Everyone who has not been redeemed through the blood of Jesus is justifiably under the penalty of sin and judgment.

Every believer who has been redeemed by the power of the blood must remember what life was like before he or she was washed in the waters of Grace through faith in Jesus Christ. Paul reminds us in Ephesians the second chapter of our former condition before the blood of Jesus redeemed us.

> *And you hath he quickened who were dead in trespasses and sins; wherein in time past ye walked according to the course of the world, according to the prince of the power of the air.*
> *Ephesians 2:1-2*

We sometimes forget where we came from and fail to give thanks to God for bringing us to a new state of living. It would serve us well to remember the words of Isaiah 51:1

> *Hearken to me, ye that follow after righteousness, ye that seek the Lord: look unto the rock whence ye are hewn, and to the hole of the pit whence ye are digged.*

When we look back at the pit of death from which He delivered us, we express both private and public gratitude. If we find that our expressions of gratitude are false and not genuine we need only to look again into the pit from which we have been pulled. When I read Ephesians 2, I am reminded of a once popular movie called "Dead Men Walking." It is an irrefutable fact that an unregenerate person gravitates to dead things. He seeks entertainment in dead media, and rushes after peace in dead substance abuse. He clamors for emotional fulfillment in dead relationships. Paul accurately explained that we were dead in our sins, not only because we were born in sin, but because we live and walk in a sinful lifestyle. Our words were dead, our deeds were dead, and our appearance was that of a spiritually dead person.

> *When you were dead in your sins and in the uncircumcision of your flesh, God made you alive through the blood of Christ. He forgave us all our sins. Having canceled the charge of our legal indebtedness, which stood against us and condemned us; he has taken it away, nailing it to the cross.*
> *Colossians 2:13-14*

In Ephesians 2:2 Paul uses the word "walked" inferring a course of deliberate direction; a course that every man who is born of a woman inherently pursues. It infers that we not only sin occasionally, but that we are involved in a habitual practice of sin. It implies that our practice of sin is innate corruption and alienation from God. We should always remember that the wages of sin is death.

> *There is a way that seemeth right unto a man, but the end thereof are the ways of death.*
> *Proverbs 16:25*

We rejoice today because by the Grace of God and the power of the blood of Jesus, we walk in the newness of life and as living epistles.

> *Having therefore, brethren, boldness to enter into the holiest by the blood of Jesus, By a new and living way, which he hath consecrated for us, through the veil, that is to say, his flesh; And having a high priest over the house of God; Let us draw near with a true heart in full assurance of faith, having our hearts sprinkled from an evil conscience, and our bodies washed with pure water.*
> *Hebrews 10:19-22*

Though we are washed in the blood of Jesus and have our minds seared, we must learn how to live a life that is set apart for the cause of Christ. Living for Christ requires sanctification, and sanctification requires obedience to the Word of God. To obey involves the discipline to follow leadership. This is directly related to the bitting process spoken of by James in chapter three. It prepares us for our responsibility to walk worthily in the vocation wherein we are called. It prepares us to consider the things which leads to death through the rudiments of the flesh: the way we dress, the music we listen too, what we look at on television and on the internet, even the things we read. If we are drawn toward sin by any of these things, we should allow the blood of Jesus to purge our "conscience" from dead works.

The spirit of disobedience continues to follow us even after we have submitted to the will of God.

Death thrives on the spirit of disobedience; there was nothing inherently wrong with the fruit that Adam ate in the Garden of Eden. When God created it on the third day, He said it was good. There was nothing wrong with the place where the tree was planted on which the fruit grew, for God called it good when it was created. The sin lay not in the composition of the fruit that was eaten, but in the disobedience of the one who ate it. Adam's willingness to disobey God's clearly given instructions not to eat of the tree produced the sinful nature of the sinfulness we battle with everyday.

Paul infers that our tendency to reject God's rule to obey and to yield to the rudiments of the flesh is a spiritual attack on us; *it is the spirit that now worketh in the children of disobedience.* The truth of the matter is, this spirit of disobedience continues to follow us even after we have submitted to the will of God. That is why we, as baptized believers, should pray to God to protect us from that mindset. Death is in the desires of the flesh. In today's society when we talk about the flesh we speak of its miraculous structure, its DNA or its cellular building blocks. However, when God speaks about the flesh He refers to the wrong desires a person makes in pursuit of his or her ambitions. Paul tells us in Romans 8:13, *"If we live by the flesh, we will die by the flesh."* Paul so correctly describes the flesh by saying:

> *Among whom also we all had our conversation in time past in the lust of the flesh, fulfilling the desires of the flesh and of the mind.*
> Ephesians 2:3

Just think for a moment, if God had taken away our flesh at the time of our conversion, we would have no problem living a set apart life for Christ. Paul in Romans 8 wrote,

"But if ye through the spirit (or bitting) do mortify the deeds of the body, ye shall live."

The bitting process enables us to become more obedient to the will of God and to the visionary

Fasting is a form of spiritually bitting or subduing of the flesh. Fasting allows us to regularly kill the desires of the flesh for if we do not kill it, it will kill us. Although we were born as dead men walking, life came by the love and Grace of God. We can rejoice that spiritual death is not the final state of those who submit to the call and will of God. Verse 4 of Ephesians the second chapter starts with, "But God ..." Just as death came by Adam's disobedience, life came by Jesus Christ. God's rich mercy and love gave us life. The bitting process enables us to become more obedient to the will of God and to the visionary under whom we have been placed. It teaches us to stand fast and to be patient, not yielding to the will of the flesh, and to pray without ceasing. The bitting process is a formidable weapon when it comes to resisting the wiles of the devil.

CHAPTER EIGHT

THE MOUTH

I've always wondered why James used the bit and bridle and not the harness as a metaphor to demonstrate leadership and control in the house of God. I'm convinced that he chose the bit because of the mouth's sensitivity to the pull of the rein, but it can, in and of itself, change the course of events. Matthew 15:18 reads, *"But what comes out of the mouth comes from the heart, and this defiles a man."* Proverbs 18:21 teach that *"Death and life are in the power of the tongue:"* The mouth with a few words can destroy what took years to build. In the same sentence in which James speaks of the bit and bridle he speaks of the tongue as being unruly. James makes mention of the tongue four times and warns us that it is a fire.

> *And the tongue is a fire, a world of iniquity: so is the tongue among our members, that it defileth the whole body, and setteth on fire the course of nature; and it is set on fire of hell. For every kind of beasts, and of birds, and of serpents, and of things in the sea, is tamed, and hath been tamed of mankind: But the tongue can no man tame; it is an unruly evil, full of deadly poison.*
> James 3:6-8

In verse 5 he says that the tongue is a small member of the body and boast great things and kindles a great fire. In the previous chapter, James talks about faith and its works. He says, "faith without works is dead," and I must say, it is also unprofitable. He associates faith with making one conceited, thinking of himself as a lord over other man's heritage. Faith increases one's ability to speak more eloquently than others give him impudence to think, but those who use their faith to promote ambitious gains, James condemns and infers that they are most likely to be the ones who are guilty of kindling a sinful fire with their tongue, and should be cautioned against a dictating, censorious, mischievous use of it.

James warns us not to use our tongues so as to lord it over others: My brethren, be not many masters, etc. (James 5:1) These words do not forbid us, the church, from doing what we can to direct and instruct others in the way. Our duty as leaders in the church is to reprove the unfaithful in a Christ like manner for what is amiss. However, we must not speak and act as those who are continually assuming authority. We must not prescribe or try to persuade in such manner as to make our own sentiments or beliefs a standard by which we try others. God gives various gifts to men and expects from them according to the measure of their faith that they have developed. *"Therefore be not many masters"* (or teachers, as some read it); "do not give yourselves the air of teacher, imposer, or judges, but rather speak with humility.
(Matthew Henry's Commentary on the Whole Bible: New Modern Edition, Electronic Database. Copyright © 1991 by Hendrickson Publishers, Inc.)

Bitting helps control the body by putting pressure on the tongue.

Figuratively speaking, the tongue can be sharpened like a sword or used as a sensor like a serpent - a reference to its ability to utter caustic, poisonous words. Like a bow, the tongue can project lies, or like an arrow, can be shot out, striking down with its deceit. The tongue can be used as a weapon for attack, wounding like a sharp knife. The tongue can be used viciously for flattery, backbiting, deceit, unrestrained speech, lying, strife and cursing, destruction, and craftiness. (Ps 52:2), (Ps 64:3) (Ps 140:3) (Jer 9:3) (Jer 9:8) (Jer 18:18) (Ps 5:9; Prov 28:23) (Ps 57:4) (Ps 50:19) (Ps 15:3; Prov 25:23) (Job 15:5). (Ps 73:9), (Ps 109:2; Prov 26:28), (Ps 31:20), (Hos 7:16).

People may use the tongue to sin, or to speak of the Lord's righteousness and to sing praise to God. The tongue of the wise promotes health; the tongue of the righteous is a treasure like choice silver. The Bible speaks of keeping the tongue from evil, of guarding the tongue and of bridling it. (James 1:26) (Ps 39:1) (Ps 35:28) (Ps 126:2) (Prov 12:18) (Prov 10:20) (Ps 34:13) (Prov 21:23)

Believers who fail to bridle their tongues will find that they are always in the midst of controversy

The tongue is an indicator of a person's spirit: it reveals what is in the heart. In the classic New Testament passage on the tongue, James warns specifically against the evil of an uncontrolled and uncharitable tongue. (James 3:1-12) Copyright © 1986, Thomas Nelson Publishers)

The scripture is filled with positive affirmations that are designed to increase our faith and build our spiritual demeanor. *"I can do all things through Jesus Christ who strengthens me."*

"Call those things which be not as though they were." "Lean not to thine own understanding. In all thy ways acknowledge Him and He shall direct thy paths." We have preached a lot over the years on faith and how it can turn vision into reality. Messages like "name it and claim it" and "Profession brings possession," Romans 4:17 gives us Biblical assurance that we are right in claiming these truths.

Believers who fail to bridle their tongues will find that they are always in the midst of controversy and are a hindrance to the development of the local church ministries, and are, by all means, a thorn in the side of their church leadership. They react to the physical and base their spiritual experiences on the carnal aspects of ministry.

The tongue can lift you high, then cast you down to its lowest level; it can give you honor in one breath, then in the same breath discredit you. It makes you look good one minute, and then makes you look bad the next. It can dress you up to look presidential in one setting and then make you look naked in the next. All through the Bible the tongue has played its role in the life of man. We know that Adam was naked because he said, "I am naked." Noah said, "It's going to rain." Moses said, "Let my people go." Joshua said, "We can possess the land." With the tongue David sent for Bathsheba, and Isaiah said, "Woe is me." But what would this world be if Jesus had not said, "Father forgive them, for they know not what they do."

Bitting helps control the body by putting pressure on the tongue. Our directions may be formidable by the tongue's challenge of our path. We may be pressing full speed ahead, going where our hearts lead us to go, but by no account does it mean that we are going in the right direction. However, the leader of our ministries may choose to change the direction by pulling on the reigns. As babes in ministry we are often governed by giftedness or ambition. It takes time to learn how to live holy and to bring under subjection the rudiments of the flesh. We can't say what we want to say as babes in the Lord's church; neither can we go where we want to go. We are not our own, but are bought with a price.

Babies mimic or parody what they see and hear. As babies in the church it may not be expedient for you to do or to say what a more mature Christian does or says. Babies do not eat what adults eat, their little bodies can't process the food; therefore, likewise, there are some teachings that you, as a new convert, may not be able to endure. Be patience and submissive to leadership, and allow your local church leader to guide you through the ministry development stage. Your Christian character will carry you much farther than giftedness and ambition will ever take you. Let me close this section by saying always stop to think before you speak because words do hurt; they can kill and destroy one's character. It is hard to heal one who has been wounded by words. Even when you are angry, stop and think before you speak because words spoken in anger, although they may be forgiven, may never be forgotten.

CHAPTER NINE

PRAYERFULNESS

No life as a Christian can be complete without a commitment to prayer and supplication; prayer is the believer's most formidable weapon; it helps to subdue the most insurmountable challenges and fortifies the believer's resistance against the enemy's stronghold. Without prayer it will be impossible to submit to the bitting process.

Prayer connects us to the divine providence God has purposed for our lives. Although worship and praise puts the believer in the presence of God, prayer takes the believer where praise cannot. Prayer enables the believer to do the impossible, see the invisible and overcome the insurmountable. There are levels of anointing that accompanies prayer and ultimately put you in the favor of God. *"The effectual fervent prayer of a righteous man availeth much."* All prayers are not sincere. Some try to flatter God with fancy words and the eloquence of speech, but God measures our prayers by the purity of our intention.

Fervent Prayer is tied to the believer's faith. Without prayer we can't communicate with God and without faith we can't please Him. Faith is the foundation of the believer's relationship with God. We must believe that He is and without Him we are not. Without faith our prayers become as sounding brass and tinkling cymbals, hollow words that carry with them false expectations and a false sense of hope. Prayer discloses the believer's trust and dependence on God as the omnipotent creator. All throughout the history of the Bible prayer has been the source of deliverance for God's people, individually, as with Daniel, or collectively, as with the Hebrew Boys.

"Men should always pray and not faint." Prayer changes the image and purpose of the believer; such as was with Paul on the road to Damascus. When the church had concerns about Paul's character, the Lord said, *"He prayeth."* Prayer makes a difference. Paul's life without Christ was out of control; he had a zeal of godliness, but not according to knowledge. Paul had to submit to the bitting process (he went to a street called straight). Because of the diversity of Paul's calling, his bitting process was close-up and personal. Three years of intense guidance in the desert of Arabia.

The believer must learn how to pray and what to pray for. James 4:2 state *"...ye have not because ye ask not."* Asking or praying must be done in a proper manner. James in verse 3 infers that praying amiss or for the wrong purpose will result in unanswered prayers.

The attitude toward prayer is developed during the bitting or guidance process

Bitting teaches us what and how to pray. The attitude toward prayer is developed during the bitting or guidance process; words used and the purity of our intent will determine whether or not God's answer will be according to our expectations. It is possible to pray sincerely and not believe it when God answers. When Peter was in jail and the church prayed without for him, the church did not believe when God answered their prayer. Preaching may move the congregation and praise may move the people, but prayer moves God. As was with the church in Jerusalem, sometime God's response to our prayers are faster than we expect, but we soon learn that every encounter with God is by the power of prayer, *"The effectual fervent prayer of a righteous man availeth much."* God even answers the prayers of those who have fallen out of His favor; Genesis tells us that the Lord heard Cain's prayer after the killing of his brother, and promised revenge on anyone who would avenge Abel's death in regards toward Cain. Although Cain appeared to be out of the good graces of God, God heard his prayer immediately; when we pray we must start to look that very moment for the answer. By faith we must believe that God is able to do far greater and exceeding abundantly above all that we can ask.

> *"In my deepest, darkest moments, what really got me through was a prayer. Sometimes my prayer was 'Help me.' Sometimes a prayer was 'Thank you.' What I've discovered is that intimate connection and communication with my creator will always get me through because I know my support, my help, is just a prayer away."* Lyanla Vanzant

There are those who believe that the power of humanity is enough to eradicate poverty, sickness, and despair. They opt to build hospitals and end wars, they strive to live their lives today and not prepare for death. They blame religion and the Church for the failures of mankind, and put their trust in chariots, the sequence of cards, and the fall of the dice. As I think on these things I know from my experience with God that the answer to these aforementioned things comes through the power of prayer.

All of my life I have been exposed to ministry in one form or the other. Almost every night there was something going on at church: Sunday morning and Sunday night, Monday nights missionary meeting, Tuesday prayer meeting, Wednesday Bible class, Thursday choir practice, Friday youth fellowship, and Saturday usher board meetings. They all started and ended with prayer. In those day when we got to school every day started with prayer. Prayer was the equalizer, it seemed to settle everyone down and set the expectations for the gathering in its proper place. It was commonplace to have prayer before meals and family gatherings. Our entire lives were inundated with some form of ambience to God.

I'm almost sure that removal of prayer from the school has had an adverse effect on school violence. There are statistics that will prove that children are more or less prone to violence today than they were before the removal of prayer from the school. It was not only prayer that affected the minds of the children, it was also the songs they sang, "Yes Jesus loves me," "Joy to the world," "It came upon a midnight clear," these too had an effect on the development of our children's character. Our schools help to shape our communities, and our communities shape our nation; taking prayer from the schools meant taking it from a large portion of our community and ultimately our nation. I'm sure that the influx of foreign immigrants and exposure to new religious ideology also aided in our move from God, but as prayer brought Israel back to God, so shall it bring America and its people back to Him. As a nation or as individuals I hear God, "Blessed is the nation whose God is the Lord." As a principality God says, "except the Lord keep the city, they that watches, watches but in vain" and as a people or individual He says, "if my people, who are called by my name, will humble themselves and pray and seek my face and turn from their wicked ways, then I will hear from heaven, and I will forgive their sin and will heal their land. He has not forgotten us, and Prayer is the answer.

The answer comes through the power of prayer

There is nothing you are going through that cannot be resolved through prayer. He is able to mend broken marriages, disorderly homes, change unruly dispositions, and economic devastation. He can repair broken relationships, and reverse spirits of unforgiveness. He can change unholy desires. The healing of our minds leads to the renewing of our spirits; it puts us in a better place. David said in the 91st Psalm:

> *He that dwelleth in the secret place of the most High shall abide under the shadow of the Almighty. Surely he shall deliver thee from the snare of the fowler, and from the noisome pestilence.*
>
> *He shall cover thee with his feathers, and under his wings shalt thou trust: his truth shall be thy shield and buckler. Thou shalt not be afraid for the terror by night; nor for the arrow that flieth by day;* [6] *Nor for the pestilence that walketh in darkness; nor for the destruction that wasteth at noonday.*
>
> *A thousand shall fall at thy side, and ten thousand at thy right hand; but it shall not come nigh thee. Only with thine eyes shalt thou behold and see the reward of the*

> wicked. Because thou hast made the LORD, which is my refuge, even the most High, thy habitation;
>
> There shall no evil befall thee, neither shall any plague come nigh thy dwelling. For he shall give his angels charge over thee, to keep thee in all thy ways. They shall bear thee up in their hands, lest thou dash thy foot against a stone.
>
> Thou shalt tread upon the lion and adder: the young lion and the dragon shalt thou trample under feet. Because he hath set his love upon me, therefore will I deliver him: I will set him on high, because he hath known my name. He shall call upon me, and I will answer him: I will be with him in trouble; I will deliver him, and honour him. With long life will I satisfy him, and shew him my salvation.

Let's look at one of the most referred to prayers in the Bible, the prayer of Jabez:

> *Jabez cried out to the God of Israel, "Oh that you would bless me and enlarge my territory! Let your hand be with me, and keep me from harm so that I will be free from pain." And God granted his request. 1 Chronicles 4:10*

How much more could he have put into the prayer? It encompassed the whole spectrum of omnipotence as it relates to one's personal self.

Prayer can be as short and compact as the prayer of Jabez; they may also be long, inclusive, and eloquently structured as Solomon's prayer at the dedication of the temple:

> *Then Solomon stood before the altar of the LORD in front of the whole assembly of Israel, spread out his hands toward heaven [23] and said: LORD, the God of Israel, there is no God like you in heaven above or on earth below— you who keep your covenant of love with your servants who continue wholeheartedly in your way. [24] You have*

kept your promise to your servant David my father; with your mouth you have promised and with your hand you have fulfilled it—as it is today.

[25] Now LORD, the God of Israel, keep for your servant David my father the promises you made to him when you said, 'You shall never fail to have a successor to sit before me on the throne of Israel, if only your descendants are careful in all they do to walk before me faithfully as you have done.' [26] And now, God of Israel, let your word that you promised your servant David my father come true.

[27] But will God really dwell on earth? The heavens, even the highest heaven, cannot contain you. How much less this temple I have built! [28] Yet give attention to your servant's prayer and his plea for mercy, LORD my God. Hear the cry and the prayer that your servant is praying in your presence this day. [29] May your eyes be open toward this temple night and day, this place of which you said, 'My Name shall be there,' so that you will hear the prayer your servant prays toward this place. [30] Hear the supplication of your servant and of your people Israel when they pray toward this place. Hear from heaven, your dwelling place, and when you hear, forgive.

[31] When anyone wrongs their neighbor and is required to take an oath and they come and swear the oath before your altar in this temple, [32] then hear from heaven and act. Judge between your servants, condemning the guilty by bringing down on their heads what they have done, and vindicating the innocent by treating them in accordance with their innocence.

[33] When your people Israel have been defeated by an enemy because they have sinned against you, and when they turn back to you and give praise to your name, praying and making supplication to you in this temple, [34] then hear from heaven and forgive the sin of your people Israel and bring them back to the land you gave to their ancestors.

[35] When the heavens are shut up and there is no rain because your people have sinned against you, and when

they pray toward this place and give praise to your name and turn from their sin because you have afflicted them, ³⁶ then hear from heaven and forgive the sin of your servants, your people Israel. Teach them the right way to live, and send rain on the land you gave your people for an inheritance.

³⁷ When famine or plague comes to the land, or blight or mildew, locusts or grasshoppers, or when an enemy besieges them in any of their cities, whatever disaster or disease may come, ³⁸ and when a prayer or plea is made by anyone among your people Israel—being aware of the afflictions of their own hearts, and spreading out their hands toward this temple— ³⁹ then hear from heaven, your dwelling place. Forgive and act; deal with everyone according to all they do, since you know their hearts (for you alone know every human heart), ⁴⁰ so that they will fear you all the time they live in the land you gave our ancestors.

⁴¹ As for the foreigner who does not belong to your people Israel but has come from a distant land because of your name— ⁴² for they will hear of your great name and your mighty hand and your outstretched arm—when they come and pray toward this temple, ⁴³ then hear from heaven, your dwelling place. Do whatever the foreigner asks of you, so that all the peoples of the earth may know your name and fear you, as do your own people Israel, and may know that this house I have built bears your Name.

⁴⁴ When your people go to war against their enemies, wherever you send them, and when they pray to the LORD toward the city you have chosen and the temple I have built for your Name, ⁴⁵ then hear from heaven their prayer and their plea, and uphold their cause.

⁴⁶ When they sin against you—for there is no one who does not sin—and you become angry with them and give them over to their enemies, who take them captive to their own lands, far away or near; ⁴⁷ and if they have a change of heart in the land where they are held captive, and repent and plead with you in the land of their captors and say, 'We have sinned, we have done wrong, we have acted wickedly'; [48] *and if they turn back to you with all their heart and soul in the land of their enemies who took them captive, and pray to you toward the land you gave their ancestors, toward the city you have chosen and the temple I have built for your Name;* [49] *then from heaven, your dwelling place, hear their prayer and their plea, and uphold their cause.* [50] *And forgive your people, who have sinned against you; forgive all the offenses they have committed against you, and cause their captors to show them mercy;* [51] *for they are your people and your inheritance, whom you brought out of Egypt, out of that iron-smelting furnace.*

[52] *May your eyes be open to your servant's plea and to the plea of your people Israel, and may you listen to them whenever they cry out to you.* [53] *For you singled them out from all the nations of the world to be your own inheritance, just as you declared through your servant Moses when you, Sovereign* LORD, *brought our ancestors out of Egypt. 1Kings 8:22—61*

Does it mean that Jabez's prayer was less favorable to God because it was shorter and covered fewer concerns than Solomon's prayer? It certainly does not. God honors prayers according to the purity of their intent.

As a child I remember hearing my grandmother pray. Her prayers always seemed simple and inclusive; she seemed to, in a few words, remember everybody: neighbors, family, circumstances, and promises. I don't remember her asking for material thing, but rather she asked for good health and guidance through tough times. As wicked as my grandfather was (I guess I could find a better word than wicked), I never saw my grandfather in church, but I remember that he cursed a lot, and I do remember him praying, and God must have answered his prayers because although my grandfather could not read he had a great sense for business. He owned a "night club", negotiated with the army to take their surplus barracks and bring them from Miami to Pompano on a truck, he sharecropped but never went to the field, raised hogs, owned a truck, a car, and bus. He never went to town as far as I know, but he trusted in God and prayed for God to bring the family through tough times.

CHAPTER TEN

LEADERSHIP

In today's Church respect for leadership is a rare quality. This exists because the people who want and demand respect outnumber the people who are willing to give it. However, Jesus more than 2,000 years ago prescribed a remedy for what has been and still is today, a thorn in the side of church leadership. When it comes to leadership there are two popular portions of scripture that comes to mind, "obey them that have rule over you," and "do unto others as you would have them to do unto you."

We show respect by showing genuine and positive regard for leaders, by listening to them and giving them our undivided attention, by acknowledging them as valuable parts of ministries and in the development of our Christian character. The bitting process enhances our ability to show respect for leadership. Withholding or manipulating positive and genuine response to our leaders shows absolute disrespect for leadership. When disrespect for leadership goes unchecked it becomes contempt, and contempt then becomes full blown hatred.

Disrespect is so ingrained in our ministries and churches that it has raised its ugly head even among leaders. God expects us as leaders in the Lord's Church to be guided by the Holy Spirit and to embrace godly ordained order in accordance with God's Divine Authority. Leaders who have not endured a godly bitting process find it difficult to submit to a spirit of cooperation among peers and show respect toward senior leaders.

> *Let every soul be subject unto the higher powers. For there is no power but of God: the powers that be are ordained of God.* ² *Whosoever therefore resisteth the power, resisteth the ordinance of God: and they that resist shall receive to themselves damnation.* ³ *For rulers are not a terror to good works, but to the evil. Wilt thou then not be afraid of the power? Do that which is good, and thou shalt have praise of the same:*
> Romans 13:1-3

In Disrespect: "Negation of Authority" Basilea Schlink offered this explanation for the root cause of disrespect: *"Why is it so difficult for us to respect people who deserve to be respected? Why is it especially truth in our time, even among Christians, that people take such a stand against respect and authority? Why is it difficult for us to recognize the words of scripture and to regard them as binding for us in our everyday life... because we are so filled with our own importance and our own honor. The proud cannot humble themselves easily... if I respect God,*

I also have to respect those whom he has appointed to be over me, in spite of their deficiencies and mistakes.

Much of what I write and have learned over the years I've learned by attending Sunday school and from the text we use printed by Word Aflame Book Publishers. There are many forms of leadership, but I have discovered that each one manifests the following characteristics.

1. Leaders can influence and control the behavior of other people by their words, experiences, and force of personality.
2. Leaders can relate to others and persuade them to follow their directions and orders.
3. Leaders Foster a spirit of cooperation among others that result in completion of tasks.

Paul in I Timothy 3:1-7, outlines the qualifications for one kind of leader, the bishop: Blameless - He must be a person of unquestionable character. Husband of one wife - He must be the husband of only one wife (if he is married). Vigilant - He stands watch over those whom he serves guarding them against danger and harm and so on. (Read the chapter.)

The bitting process solidifies the believer's stand in the doctrine of the church

In the New Testament there are other requirements for godly leadership; it also infers that God holds leaders to a higher standard of holiness than their followers. The standard for godly leaders are higher because of the tremendous responsibility God placed on them. Their charge is to lead the church in a spiritual path to higher levels of commitment and service. Paul declared the purpose of godly leadership is *"the perfecting of the saints, for the work of the ministry, for the edification of the body of Christ."*

The bitting process solidifies the believer's stand in the doctrine of the church referred to by most as the "Apostolic Doctrine." Paul wrote to Timothy *"Now the spirit speaketh expressly..."* The danger of departing from the faith can be seen in Paul's concluding words in the same chapter; *"Take heed unto thyself, and unto the doctrine..."*

> Now the Spirit speaketh expressly, that in the latter times some shall depart from the faith, giving heed to seducing spirits, and doctrines of devils; ²Speaking lies in hypocrisy; having their conscience seared with a hot iron; ³Forbidding to marry, and commanding to abstain from meats, which God hath created to be received with thanksgiving of them which believe and know the truth.
> I Timothy 4:1-3.

> Take heed unto thyself, and unto the doctrine; continue in them: for in doing this thou shalt both save thyself, and them that hear thee.
> I Timothy 4:16

Departing from the faith (the Apostolic Doctrine) endangers our relationship with God, our salvation, and the salvation of those who are connected to us. As baptized believers, we should reject any teaching that minimizes the role of the Holy Spirit in our lives. There are five doctrines that are embraced by us as believers: The Doctrine of Justification, Sanctification, Divine Healing, Second Coming of Christ, and the Doctrine of the Baptism with the Holy Spirit with the Initial Evidence of Speaking in Tongues.

As we embrace each of these doctrines and incorporate them as essential parts of our visionary purposes, we know that they must also become the focus of our congregations. The burden of turning our visions into reality must become their burden.

Each member of the congregation must partner with the leadership of the church and with the visionary (the pastor). The Pastor, after a process of training which includes a period of bridling and bitting, must evaluate the worthiness of both spiritual and personal Christian development of each member of the congregation, then empower them as partners of the vision.

What God gives us as visionaries is not some private ambitious quest to be fulfilled for our own glory, but a spiritual blueprint, designed by God for the spiritual and personal development of His people, the Church, the Bride of Christ. Jesus empowered His disciples and sent them out two-by-two. Once this was established it adopted this practice; Paul and Barnabas (Acts 11:30), Barnabas and Mark (Acts 15:39), Paul and Silas (Acts 15:40. With the power of God on their lives and their hearts filled with faith in Jesus Christ they must have been the most affective dynamic apostolic teams ever formed.

> *Then the disciples, every man according to his ability, determined to send relief unto the brethren which dwelt in Judaea: Which also they did, and sent it to the elders by the hands of Barnabas and Saul.*
> *Acts 11:29-30*

> *So when they were dismissed, they came to Antioch: and when they had gathered the multitude together, they delivered the epistle: ³¹which when they had read, they rejoiced for the consolation. ³²And Judas and Silas, being prophets also themselves, exhorted the brethren with many words, and confirmed them. ³³And after they had tarried there a space, they were let go in peace from the brethren unto the Apostles. ³⁴Notwithstanding it pleased Silas to abide there still. ³⁵Paul also and Barnabas continued in Antioch, teaching and preaching the word of the Lord, with many others also. ³⁶And some days after Paul said unto Barnabas, let us go again and visit our brethren in every city where we have preached the word of the LORD, and see how they*

> do. ³⁷*And Barnabas determined to take with them John, whose surname was Mark.* ³⁸ *But Paul thought not good to take him with them, who departed from them from Pamphylia, and went not with them to the work.* ³⁹*And the contention was so sharp between them, that they departed asunder one from the other: and so Barnabas took Mark, and sailed unto Cyprus;* ⁴⁰*And Paul chose Silas, and departed, being recommended by the brethren unto the grace of God.*
> Acts 15:30-40

Strength is added to strength, even multiplied when God's people work together. *"And five of you shall chase a hundred, and a thousand of you shall put ten thousand to flight."* (Leviticus 26:8) Some form of this scripture appears throughout the Bible with different numbers and different circumstances.

> *And ye shall chase your enemies, and they shall fall before you by the sword. And five of you shall chase an hundred, and an hundred of you shall put ten thousand to flight: and your enemies shall fall before you by the sword. For I will have respect unto you, and make you fruitful, and multiply you, and establish my covenant with you.*
> Leviticus 26:7-9

As leaders in the Lord's Church we must adhere to the Apostles Doctrine and teach our leaders who serve under our oversight to do the same, and to understand what it means to be justified and sanctified, what it means to be divinely delivered and healed and filled with the Holy Spirit with speaking in tongues. We are targets of the enemy; Satan will do all he can to disrupt God's plan for our lives. He will sow seeds of discord among the brethren (leaders) to prevent them from reaping a mighty harvest or turning their vision into reality, but he can never destroy the effort of all. There will always be some who will betray the Lord, but there will also be the faithful who will stand the test and win the war of visionary purpose in their lives.

God has established positions of authority and leadership in every area of human interaction

Eventually there will be a day of reckoning and judgment for the disrespect toward and disobedience to God's chosen leaders. The Israelites' disrespect of Moses brought punishment and plague (Numbers 16:41). Saul's usurpation of the sacred priestly duties resulted in the loss of his kingdom (I Samuel 13:14). When Ananias and Saphira lied to their apostolic leaders, God sent swift judgment and they died (Acts 5:1-11).

> *But on the morrow all the congregation of the children of Israel murmured against Moses and against Aaron, saying, Ye have killed the people of the LORD. And it came to pass, when the congregation was gathered against Moses and against Aaron, that they looked toward the tabernacle of the congregation: and, behold, the cloud covered it, and the glory of the LORD appeared. And Moses and Aaron came before the tabernacle of the congregation. And the LORD spake unto Moses, saying, Get you up from among this congregation, that I may consume them as in a moment. And they fell upon their faces.*
> *Numbers 16:41-45*

> *And Samuel said to Saul, thou hast done foolishly: thou hast not kept the commandment of the LORD thy God, which he commanded thee: for now would the LORD have established thy kingdom upon Israel forever. But now thy kingdom shall not continue: the LORD hath sought him a man after his own heart, and the LORD hath commanded him to be captain over his people, because thou hast not kept that which the LORD commanded thee.*
> *I Samuel 13:13-14*

> *But a certain man named Ananias, with Sapphira his wife, sold a possession, ²And kept back part of the price, his wife also being privy to it, and brought a certain part, and laid it at the apostles' feet. ³But Peter said, Ananias, why hath Satan filled thine heart to lie to the Holy Ghost, and to keep back part of the price of the land? ⁴Whiles it remained, was it not thine own? and after it was sold, was it not in thine own power? why hast thou conceived this thing in thine heart? thou hast not lied unto men, but unto God. ⁵And Ananias hearing these words fell down, and gave up the ghost: and great fear came on all them that heard these things. ⁶And the young men arose, wound him up, and carried him out, and buried him. ⁷And it was about the space of three hours after, when his wife, not knowing what was done, came in ⁸And Peter answered unto her, tell me whether ye sold the land for so much? And she said, Yea, for so much. ⁹Then Peter said unto her, How is it that ye have agreed together to tempt the Spirit of the Lord? behold, the feet of them which have buried thy husband are at the door, and shall carry thee out. ¹⁰Then fell she down straightway at his feet, and yielded up the ghost: and the young men came in, and found her dead, and, carrying her forth, buried her by her husband. ¹¹And great fear came upon all the church, and upon as many as heard these things.*
> Acts 5:1-11

Satan failed, and those who follow him and fail to submit to God will also fail. Their disrespect for godly leadership will also reveal their contempt for God's sovereignty, His plan for Apostolic Order and Authority in church leadership.

> *For if God spared not the angels that sinned, but cast them down to hell, and delivered them into chains of darkness, to be reserved unto judgment; And spared not the old world, but saved Noah the eighth person, a preacher of righteousness, bringing in the flood upon the world of the ungodly; And turning the cities of Sodom and Gomorrha into ashes condemned them with an overthrow, making them an ensample unto those that after should live ungodly; And delivered just Lot,*

> *vexed with the filthy conversation of the wicked: (For that righteous man dwelling among them, in seeing and hearing, vexed his righteous soul from day to day with their unlawful deeds;) The Lord knoweth how to deliver the godly out of temptations, and to reserve the unjust unto the day of judgment to be punished: But chiefly them that walk after the flesh in the lust of uncleanness, and despise government. Presumptuous are they, selfwilled, they are not afraid to speak evil of dignities.*
>
> *Whereas angels, which are greater in power and might, bring not railing accusation against them before the Lord. But these, as natural brute beasts, made to be taken and destroyed, speak evil of the things that they understand not; and shall utterly perish in their own corruption; And shall receive the reward of unrighteousness, as they that count it pleasure to riot in the day time. Spots they are and blemishes, sporting themselves with their own deceivings while they feast with you; Having eyes full of adultery, and that cannot cease from sin; beguiling unstable souls: an heart they have exercised with covetous practices; cursed children: Which have forsaken the right way, and are gone astray, following the way of Balaam the son of Bosor, who loved the wages of unrighteousness; But was rebuked for his iniquity: the dumb ass speaking with man's voice forbad the madness of the prophet.*
> *II Peter 2:4-16*

Keep in mind that God has established positions of authority and leadership in every area of human interaction, including the church. Godly leaders are all called to minister and serve the church in a variety of capacities and responsibilities. It is God's will for us to subject ourselves willingly to those over us and show proper respect to those in godly leadership. Lack of respect often comes from personal pride and an unwillingness to acknowledge others as being over us.

Disrespect for leaders leads to division and conflict, which results in God's judgment. God wants us to work together

harmoniously as a unified body under His headship to accomplish His will. Showing proper respect sets a good example for others and brings revival with more blessings.
Word Aflame, March 2013, Celebration Series

There are those who feel that spiritual and secular leadership are the same. However, spiritual leadership is vastly different from secular leadership. This generation of believers has experienced an explosion of both spiritual and secular workshops, seminars, programs and materials designed to bolster leadership based on the realization that "excellence never happens by accident and productivity never comes to the unprepared."

Leadership in the kingdom of God is of even greater importance, for although the world as we know it will one day pass away, spiritual leaders will still be leading the millennial kingdom. A careful study of the Word of God reveals that the value of leadership is paramount both in Heaven and on Earth. God is our example of the greatest leader, and the heavenly host is example of lining up under the authority of and in cooperation with godly leadership. If we are to be spiritual leaders or spiritual followers, we should heed the great example heaven provides.

> *His lord said unto him, Well done, thou good and faithful servant: thou hast been faithful over a few things, I will make thee ruler over many things: enter thou into the joy of thy lord.*
> *Matthew 25:21*

How much easier it would be to turn visions into reality in the church if the congregation and subordinate leaders would strive to work in harmony with the visionary of the church. More can be accomplished in the Lord's church when we work together and strive for the same thing. As Baptized Believers, it is our responsibility to follow our spiritual leaders and work in tandem with them and one another until the vision become reality and the harvest is completed.

Because members of our congregations as well as ordinary people's attitudes, mindsets, and passions change, we must develop leaders in our churches who both understand current thinking and have the ability to draw people together with a common purpose.

We can learn from studying the lives of the Judges that God will use those who dedicate themselves to Him and His cause. Their lives may not always measure up to God's will, but God will use them as long as they remain committed to Him.

Deborah and Barak's story illustrates that when you have leaders who are in total agreement with each other and possess a strong anointing combined with their faithful stewardship and willingness to obey God, great things can be achieved.

It is evident that God chose Deborah for a specific time in Israel's history; insecurity, economic instability, and apostasy filled the land, and because of it, the nation grew weak and under the control of foreign nations. God's timing for leadership is a great lesson for all believers to learn early in their walk with Him. We should honor, respect, and defer to whomever God places in spiritual leadership over us. Perhaps some Israelites did not appreciate or even believe it was God's plan to place a woman in authority over them, but it is certain she was the woman in that season to accomplish what God had set in motion. It is obvious from this story that God views diversity as helpful and necessary when it comes to leadership.

SECTION THREE

CHAPTER ELEVEN

SERVANT LEADERSHIP TRAITS

There are those who believe that the people of God can do better than they are doing, and that all that is needed are leaders who have vision to stir them up with power. I tend to believe that this is true, but with one other ingredient added – the Holy Ghost who gives a right spirit, a willing spirit, and a spirit of obedience. Haggai aroused the people who were satisfied with their nice homes, and encouraged them to build God's house. Ezra aroused the men who were content with their heathen wives, and encouraged them to take steps to rid themselves of their foreign wives and commit to a covenant according to the law of God. Nehemiah firstly stirred the King to allow him to go back to Jerusalem to repair the ruins of the city. After arriving there he found the people comfortable amid the ruins of the city, but he stirred up their conscious, which encouraged them to commit to his vision of rebuilding, and a well-fortified city began to rise.

Are you too easily content, and satisfied with doing less than you ought to do for the Lord? Servant leader have godly traits: They pray, they plan, they take risks, they do not view ruinous conditions as normal, and they have godly followers.

Servant Leaders pray and plan:

"If you find that what you do each day seems to have no link to any higher purpose, you probably want to rethink what you're doing. *(Ronald A. Heifetz, The Practice of Adaptive Leadership)*

Praying followed by planning followed by more praying is an excellent pattern to follow. We should pray for God's guidance before we plan. Then, once we have developed plans under His guidance, we should pray again for His power in executing the plans. To pray without planning is pointless. *"Faith without works is dead."* To plan without praying is powerless. Plans that are not in line with God's will stand a chance of failing, thus wasting a lot of time, money and effort.

Failure by leaders to communicate plans and decisions to their members is a frequent cause of misunderstanding in churches. And yet, there are times when leaders may feel it wise to delay announcing certain plans. For example, a leader may delay presenting a project until it is known how much it will cost, how long it will take, and similar details. This is not a secret agenda on the part of leadership, but a careful examination of the plan. Nehemiah did not reveal his plans until he considered them from all angles.

Commit thy works unto the LORD, and thy thoughts shall be established. Proverbs 16:3

Servant Leaders take risks:

God's invisible hand is always present to guide us through difficulties. Nehemiah knew he was taking a risk by approaching the king about rebuilding Jerusalem. Esther knew she was taking a risk by going before the king without being summoned. If ever you are hesitant to take risks in your leadership position, be energized and encouraged by Esther or Nehemiah. Accepting the challenge placed before you allows God's hand to guide you through whatever difficulties you may encounter. "God will never take you to a place in ministry where you are forced to retreat."

Servant Leaders should not view ruinous conditions as normal conditions:

It was nearly ninety years after being back in Jerusalem before the post exilic Jews began to consider rebuilding the wall. They had passed by the ruins day after day and had come to view the wall's ruinous condition as normal condition. Do you view empty pews on Sunday morning as normal? Visitors should be viewed as potential members. Is there satisfaction in offerings that barely cover the regular church expenses? Is it normal in your church that there are few, if any, young people present on Sunday morning? If these are "normal conditions" then your church is surviving and not thriving and the successful days of operation may be numbered unless leadership makes a conscientious effort to reverse the perceived idea of normalcy.

Servant Leaders have godly followers:

One confirming factor of leaders is that they have followers. In fact, leaders and followers are like a horse and buggy, you can't have one without the other. Your "follow-ship" confirms your leadership.

Michael Youssef, author of "The Leadership Style of Jesus" points out that the Gospels offer seven distinct confirmations that Jesus was truly the Messiah.

The first proof Jesus offered to confirm his leadership role is the witness of God the Father.

> *"And the Father himself, which hath sent me, hath borne witness of me." John 5:37a.*

The second witness was John the Baptist.

The opening chapter of John's gospel reveals the testimony.

> *And John bare record, saying, I saw the Spirit descending from heaven like a dove, and it abode upon him. And I knew him not: but he that sent me to baptize with water, the same said unto me, upon whom thou shalt see the Spirit descending, and remaining on him, the same is he which baptizeth with the Holy Ghost. And I saw, and bare record that this is the Son of God.*
> *John 1:32-34*

The Third witness of Jesus is the Works of Jesus.

> *But I have greater witness than that of John: for the works which the Father hath given me to finish, the same works that I do, bear witness of me that the Father hath sent me.*
> *John 5:36*

The fourth Witness: The Holy Spirit

> *The Spirit of the Lord is upon me, because he hath anointed me to preach the gospel to the poor; he hath sent me to heal the broken-hearted, to preach deliverance to the captives, and recovering of sight to the blind, to set at liberty them that are bruised; to preach the acceptable year of the Lord.*
> *Luke 4:18-19*

Fifth Witness: The Scriptures

> *Search the scriptures; for in them ye think ye have eternal life: and they are they which testify of me. And ye will not come to me, that ye might have life.*
> *John 5:39-40*

Sixth Witness: Miracles

The ministry of Jesus was confirmed by the miracles he performed. John's gospel refers to them as "signs" because they point to Jesus' divine nature. John records seven such signs: changing water into wine (2:1-11), healing a man's son (4:46-54), healing a lame man (5:1-9), multiplying bread and fish (6:1-14), walking on water (6:15-21), healing a blind man (9:1-7), and raising Lazarus (11:38-44). The signs John mentions bare witness to the purpose power, and leadership authority of Jesus.

The Seventh Witness: The Disciples

> *When Jesus came into the coasts of Caesarea Phlippi, he asked his disciples, saying,' whom do men say that I the Son of man am?' And they said, some say that thou art John the Baptist: some, Elias; and others, Jeremias, or one of the prophets. He saith unto them, but whom say ye that I am? And Simon Peter answered and said, Thou art the Christ, the Son of the living God. And Jesus*

answered and said unto him, Blessed art thou Simon Barjona; for flesh and blood hath not revealed it unto thee, but my Father which is in heaven. And I say also unto thee, that thou art Peter, and upon this rock I will build my church; and the gates of hell shall not prevail against it."
Matthew 16:13-18

CHAPTER TWELVE

PROFILES OF HIGHLY EFFECTIVE SERVANT LEADERS

Leaders do what's right even if it means standing alone. God instructed King Saul through the prophet Samuel to destroy Amalek and all that they had. He was to spare nothing and no one. However, Saul disobeyed the word of the LORD and spared the life of Agag. Therefore, Samuel sent for Agag and said:

> *As thy sword hath made women childless, so shall thy mother be childless among women...*
> *I Samuel 15:33*

Nehemiah was an exemplary leader. He trusted in God and prayed earnestly. He planned and was devoted to the task. He did not demand that the people take on the task of rebuilding, but he gently persuaded them. Nehemiah saw the potential of having the walls of Jerusalem rebuilt. He convinced the people that an improved city would benefit them, be good for the Jewish nation, and would be for the glory of God. Nehemiah led by example. He was always among the workers encouraging them so well that they had "a mind to work." He took risks as well as precaution so that the workers were not in danger of threats made against them while at the same time boosting moral so that the work would not be halted.

Church members (the sheep) should not be commanded from afar. They are to be gently led by their leader (the shepherd). Jesus, the "chief shepherd" called others to follow Him, and then led the way by example. Likewise, leadership of elders should not be by dogmatic rule, but by example. Nehemiah had a gifted ability to lead well; however, it was God's plan to rebuild not Nehemiah's. Although Nehemiah was the leader/vessel to oversee the vision the wall was built by eager followers who decided to forego their comfort and take on hard work until the job was completed.

Spiritual bitting eliminates the feeling of being tossed to and fro

One of the problems we have in the church today is that its leaders have not been effectively trained. This results in stunted growth for the leader as well as for the congregation. Church leaders are to be mature. They must have endured the "spiritual bitting" necessary to lead with a Christ-like character. It is hoped that through years of experience they will have not only gained the ability to lead well, but also have shown their gifted ability so clearly that church members will place unwavering confidence in them. Spiritual bitting eliminates the feeling of being tossed to and fro, of not knowing what to do, why you are doing or not doing it, and when to do or not to do it.

Cultivate The Spirit of Follow-ship.

Can the spirit of follow-ship be cultivated in our churches? The answer to that question is a resounding YES if it is kept in mind that we are all followers. Jesus Christ is ultimately the only leader. Those who would lead as pastors, ministers, elders, or teachers or in any other leadership capacity must demonstrate first of all that they follow Christ. It is important that leaders make it their aim to lead where Christ would lead. Their own visions of what the church should be and their own opinions as to what is best for the congregation must be subordinate to what Christ wants. Paul wrote to the Corinthians, "Be ye followers of me, even as I also am of Christ." Leaders must demonstrate through prayer that they rely on God's Word and His power as their primary tools in fulfilling their responsibilities. Church members will be more likely to follow a leader who humbly relies on these capabilities.

Work The Vision Like It Is Yours!

Godly leadership is critical to God's purpose for His people. Godly leaders require godly followers who are committed and who have a mind to work the vision. The vision may have been given to the pastor, but work it like it's yours. The vision may have been given to the president of the Mother's or Deacon Board, but as a member of the board, work it like it's yours. The program may have been given by the usher board president, or by the choir president or maybe by the new member of the praise team to raise funds for the church, but as a dedicated member of the body of Christ, work it like it's yours. Work it like it's yours "for the edification of the body of Christ, for the perfecting of the saints" to the glory of God!

> *And whatsoever ye do, do it heartily, as to the Lord, and not unto men; Knowing that of the Lord ye shall receive the reward of the inheritance: for ye serve the Lord Christ.*
> *Colossians 3:23-24*

The vision was given to Moses but the execution to Bezaleel and his workers. When God gave instruction to Moses for the building of the tabernacle, He said:

> *See, I have called by name Bezaleel the son of Uri, the son of Hur, the tribe of Judah: And I have filled him with the spirit of God, in wisdom, and in understanding, and in knowledge, and in all manner of workmanship,*

> *To devise cunning works, to work in gold, and in silver, and in brass, And in cutting of stones, to set them, and in carving of timber, to work in all manner of workmanship. And I, behold, have given with him Aholiab, the son of Ahisamach, of the tribe of Dan: and in the hearts of all that are wise hearted I have put wisdom, that they may make all that I have commanded thee;*

> *The tabernacle of the congregation, and the ark of the testimony, and the mercy seat that is thereupon, and all the furniture of the tabernacle,*

> *And the table and his furniture, and the pure candlestick with all his furniture, and the altar of incense, And the altar of burnt-offering with all his furniture, and the laver and his foot, And the cloths of service, and the holy garments for Aaron the priest, and the garments of his sons, to minister in the priest's office, And the anointing oil, and sweet incense for the holy place: according to all that I have commanded thee shall they do.*
> *Exodus 31:2-11*

Godly followers must have the same mind as their servant leader. In addition to working the vision and being faithful to the assignment of the leader, followers are enhancing their capabilities to step into a leadership role. Jesus instructed his disciples (followers) to watch as well as pray. Followers should watch closely the kingdom building principles of their leader. Learn how the leader interacts with people from all walks of life. Learn how the leader is able to affect result, promote unity and persevere in spite of opposition. Study leadership styles of biblical leaders such as Nehemiah, Ezra, Daniel and especially Jesus.

Embrace the Unknown

> *By faith Noah, being warned of God of things not seen as yet, moved with fear, prepared an ark to the saving of his house; by the which he condemned the world, and became heir of righteousness which is by faith. By faith Abraham, when he was called to go out into a place which he should after receive for an inheritance, obeyed; and he went out, not knowing whither he went. Hebrews 11:7-8*

Endure In Spite Of Circumstances

Jeremiah suffered because of his prophecies. He was beaten, imprisoned, considered a traitor, and mocked. In spite of it all, Jeremiah showed faith and obeyed God when doing so seemed foolish to others. He trusted God's promises of a new future for his people.

Leaders have visions that sustain them through difficult times. Ezekiel's prophecies about the destruction of Jerusalem caused friction among the Jews who were with him in Babylon. However, after the destruction his prophecies became hope to the exilic Jews for future restoration and comfort in their homeland.

Take Risks

When Esther's uncle Mordecai refused to bow before Haman as the king had commanded all the servants to do, Haman became angry. He then sought to destroy all the Jews of king Ahasuerus' kingdom because he knew that Mordecai was a Jew. Mordecai sent word to Queen Esther that Haman was plotting to kill all Jews. Esther devised a plan to save her people. According to the King's law, no one was to come before the king unless summoned by him. Although Esther had not been called to come before the king, she risked being put to death for her people's sake. She said, "

> *So will I go in unto the king, which is not according to the law: and if I perish, I perish."*
> *Esther 5:16*

Not Afraid Of Giants

David said (of Goliath), *"who is this uncircumcised Philistine, that he should defy the armies of the living God?"* David took five smooth stones to slay the Philistine giant, but it only required one to get the job done.

Maintain Their Resolve Without Regard For Consequences

Daniel stayed true to God and prayed three times a day. He refused to bow to idols, and would not eat the food or drink King Nebuchadnezzar had provided for him and his three Jewish friends. As a result of Daniel's request not to be given the king's provisions, he and his friends ate only vegetables and drank water. Through this show of unyielding resolve, God gave them favor. Daniel was given the ability to interpret dreams and see into the future.

Operate Under The Boldness Of The Holy Spirit

John was filled with the Holy Spirit from his mother's womb and his messages were boldly declared to be from God. When he saw superficial Jews coming to him to be baptized, he rebuked them: *"O generation of vipers, who hath warned you to flee from the wrath to come?"* John believed in the sanctity of marriage and boldly warned Herod Antipas that it was not lawful to have his brother's wife. This boldly declared message ultimately cost John his life.

Leaders Are Servants

> *And supper being ended, the devil having now put into the heart of Judas Iscariot, Simon's son, to betray him; Jesus knowing that the Father had given all things into his hands, and that he was from God, and went to God; He riseth from supper, and laid aside his garments; and took a towel and girded himself. After that he poureth water into a bason, and began to wash the disciples' feet, and to wipe them with the towel wherewith he was girded.*
> John 13:2-5

Leaders Recover From Failure

Jimmy Swaggart Then and Now:

THEN: Jimmy Swaggart's fall from grace in 1988 sent a shock wave throughout the Swaggart ministry. Swaggart did not confess to any specific transgression but did admit to an encounter with a New Orleans prostitute. Confronted by pictures of himself and a prostitute, he reportedly admitted in a 10 hour long session with church elders, that he had paid her to perform pornographic acts, and that he had had a fascination with pornography since childhood. The Fall of Jimmy Swaggart by Joanne Kaufman, Sex Scandals, March 7, 1988, Vol. 29-No.9, From People Magazine Archive People.com/people/archive/article/0,20098413,00.html

NOW: Rev. Swaggart is the Pastor of Family Worship Center in Baton Rouge Louisiana, a multi-cultural, interdenominational Full Gospel Church that continues to be the spiritual hub of the ministry. Thousands of lives are touched in the three camp meeting services held each year, while the weekly services continue to grow under a fresh anointing of the Holy Spirit.
Jimmy Swaggart Ministries © 2015.

Satan cannot stop the plan of God.

> *For I know the thoughts that I think toward you, saith the Lord, thoughts of peace and not of evil, to give you an expected end.*
> *Jeremiah 29:11*

Passionate For What They Believe In

The Apostle Paul was without fear when the opportunity presented itself to share the gospel, wherever he might be. He did not consider the trouble it would put him in. There was nothing as important as proclaiming the gospel. Before his Damascus road encounter, Paul, who was originally known as Saul was dedicated to or had a passion for the persecution of Christians. His passion changed dramatically after his Damascus road encounter with Jesus. The Bible says, *"and straightway he preached Christ in the synagogues, that he is the Son of God." Acts 9:20*

The Francis A. Schaeffer Institute of Church Leadership Development has this to say about the profile of Servant Leadership – "We usually know what the world calls us to, but do you know what God calls you to do? The Bible calls us to a higher level of excellence: one of vision, love, integrity, and functionality. That is what I call "incarnational leadership." It simply means that I will lead the way Christ led. I will not lead the way the world wants me to. Incarnational represents

the view that we are to leave the ways of the world and its ways of leadership, and turn to the ways of Christ. As he was incarnational, we can be too."
Church Leadership.org, The Francis A. Schaeffer Institute of Church Leadership Development.

Agents Of Change

Leadership positions affect development and stability. They are non-static. It is not possible to lead if things stay the same. If things stay the same under your leadership, you have ceased to be a leader and have become a manager, overseeing what your predecessor has already put in place. Managers are less likely to be agents of change because that is not within their sphere of responsibility. Leaders steer the horse in new directions. They inspire followers to pursue the vision for the church with energetic resilience and enthusiasm. Managers simply manage plans set in place by the visionary. They assure things run smoothly and meet established deadlines.

Jack Dunigan, author of "The Practical Leader" states that there are times when change moves faster and covers more ground than other times. Without doubt today's leaders face generational differences that are more pronounced, encounter technological advances that are more consequential, and must cope with an evolving marketplace than perhaps at any other time. Being able to bounce back, being able to go with the flow without being carried under the current is one of the most critical capacities of an effective leader."
Jack Dunigan – The Practical Leader.com, "Extend your Reach, Multiply your Effectiveness, Divide Your Work," March, 2015.

Are Agents Of Encouragement

Upon studying the history of the Israelites, we see the love, compassion and longsuffering of God displayed toward them time and time again. The Israelites promised Moses that they would obey the statues and instructions of God, but soon weakened in their faith and became disobedient, even to the point of becoming apostate. They fell from God's grace, but not from his protective covering. Although He pronounced doom and gloom upon them through prophets such as Isaiah and Jeremiah, God never turned his back on His chosen people. During their decreed captivity they experienced extreme hardship but God never left them. He gave them leaders to encourage and comfort them.

Jeremiah was instructed by God to purchase ruined property in Jerusalem to encourage the exiles that they would return. The prophet Hosea ministered in the northern kingdom of Israel during the chaotic period just before their fall. Although the prophet's messages were judgment against the nations of Israel and Judah, he singled out the northern kingdom for its gross sin and immorality. However, Hosea's prophetic messages ended on a positive note. The prophet reminds the nation of God's undying love. In spite of their unfaithfulness, He is determined to redeem them and restore them to their favored place as His Covenant People.

During Judah's captivity Daniel was given a vision that Judah would be restored to its homeland after their period of captivity that was revealed to him as a period of 70 weeks. The destruction of the Jerusalem temple was emotionally devastating to the exiled Judah therefore Ezekiel's vision of an Altar offered hope and restoration.

Constantine the Great was the Roman emperor from AD 306 to 337. During a time of unrest and civil war, he found himself leading an army against a larger force that had occupied Rome. The climactic battle fought at Milvian Bridge on October 28, 312, was a decisive victory for Constantine, putting him firmly on the path to being uncontested as emperor.

The victory also led the pagan Constantine to be the first emperor of the Roman Empire to embrace Christianity. According to church historian Eusebius of Caesarea, this came about because of a vision Constantine allegedly had from Christ on the day before the battle. The claimed vision was that of the *Chi-Rho*, the first two letters of the word *Christ* in Greek, superimposed. This "trophy of a cross of light in the heavens" bore the inscription "Conquer by this." Constantine did just that, after putting the *Chi-Rho* on the banner of his army.
James B. North, Standard Lesson Commentary (2016-2017)

The Bible clearly establishes that God uses visions and dreams to communicate (Genesis 41:15; Numbers 12:6). In Acts Chapter nine, God uses a vision of one man (Ananias) to explain the vision of another man (Saul).

> And there was a certain disciple at Damascus, named Ananias; and to him said the Lord in a vision, Ananias. And he said, Behold, I am here, Lord. And the Lord said unto him, Arise, and go into the street which is called Straight, and enquire in the house of Judas for one called Saul, of Tarsus: for behold he prayeth. And hath seen in a vision a man named Ananias coming in, and putting his hand on him, that he might receive his sight.
> *Acts 9:10-12*

God continues to speak. He continues to give visions to leaders of the church. Those who have been faithful, who have begun preparing and continues to prepare themselves for leadership service to God's people, are hearing from God. These servant leaders have taken hold of the reins of the spiritual bit with determination to drive and go forward.

> *God, who at sundry times and in divers manners spake in time past unto the fathers by the prophets, hath in these last days spoken unto us by his Son...*
> *Hebrews 1:1-2*

Determine Your Level of Adaptability

At what level do you most often think? At what level are you most often called upon to think? Do you find yourself mind multitasking? Is your daily "to do task" list long and detailed or limited and general? Your thinking level determines your leadership level. Depending upon how well you have embraced the bitting process will determine how well equipped you are to adapt to change and deal with swift transitions that will inevitably take place.

CHAPTER THIRTEEN

MAKE A DIFFERENCE

Nehemiah saw the problems that existed in Jerusalem and he moved to make a difference; he also led by example. He was always among the workers, encouraging them so well that they had "a mind to work". They built the wall despite opposition.

"According to the United States Census Bureau, (2015) the world population was slightly above seven billion. Because of this enormous population, many issues affect our world. Worldwide, we see major problems – hunger, human rights violations, discrimination, homelessness, and poverty – that seem too massive to solve. Furthermore, many widows and orphans are ignored.

Although these world issues seem overwhelming, God's people should not close their eyes to them. Several questions should come to mind concerning these mammoth, worldwide problems. What should be our attitude toward human issues? What can we do? What should we do?

Jesus was confronted by a lawyer in Luke 10:25-29. The lawyer inquired about gaining eternal life. Jesus responded to the lawyer by asking him the contents of the law. The lawyer's response was that a person was to love God and his neighbor. Jesus affirmed his response. Our Saviour then told the man to live out the love for God and his neighbor. Trying to justify his actions, the lawyer asked who was his neighbor. Jesus proceeds to tell the parable of the Good Samaritan.

In Luke 10:30-37, Jesus told of a man who had been beaten and robbed. The man was helpless and hurting. A traveling priest saw the man but avoided contact by walking to the other side of the road. Next, a Levite saw him but he too provided no assistance and proceeded to walk on the other side.

Finally, a Samaritan came and saw this man. His heart was moved to take action. He nursed the man's wounds and set him on his beast. The Samaritan took him to a local inn so that he could recover. He established a tab with the innkeeper to absorb all the injured man's expenses.

From this parable, we see a man who was compassionate. During that era, Samaritans and Jews were on hostile terms, but the Samaritan did not let ethnic differences affect his Christian responsibility to care for this man.

Today, God wants his people not to ignore the plight of the marginalized and oppressed. Christians must not be self-absorbed. We are called to be light in dark places (Matt. 5:16). Christians can ill-afford to have the attitude the disciples exhibited when they told Jesus to send the multitude away hungry (Mark 6:35-36). Our attitude must be one of compassion, love, and unselfishness.

God calls us to action. Isaiah 1:17 tell us, *"Learn to do well; seek judgment, relieve the oppressed, judge the fatherless, plead for the widow."*

When dilemmas are before us, we should not sit idly by and ignore them. Prayer is the starting point. Through prayer, we can obtain specifics on what to do with the dilemmas around us. It is important to note that God does not assign every human issue as an individual assignment to us. For instance, He may not assign you the direct responsibility of working with orphans. Yet He may ask you to financially contribute to a ministry that specializes in that area.

Above all, we must each have a heart to help others. When we have a compassionate heart, we are driven to help others. So what can we do? First, we can allow the love of God to flow through us. First John 3:18 states, *"My little children, let us not love in word, neither in tongue; but in deed and in truth."* "Love" is an action word. It is more than affection or verbal expressions. It is doing.

There is a story about two birds. One bird was in a cherry tree, and the other bird was on the ground with a broken wing. The bird in the tree was eating cherries and telling the injured bird, "I love you; I love you." The injured bird looked up at the bird in the tree and said, "If you love me, send down some cherries!" Love is more than talk; it is action.

We too can be unselfish. Our Saviour demonstrated selflessness. His life reflected sacrifice. Jesus left heaven to come to earth. He could easily have stayed in heaven's comfort, but He thought more about others. When Jesus arrived on earth, He ministered. His ministry consisted of helping and serving others. This was reflected as He healed the sick, fed the hungry, and encouraged the brokenhearted. Ultimately, He gave His life to save the world. (John 3:16)

In Luke 4:18-19, He uttered His life's mission: *"The Spirit of the Lord is upon me, because he hath anointed me to preach the gospel to the poor; he hath sent me to heal the brokenhearted, to preach deliverance to the captives, and recovering of sight to the blind, to set at liberty them that are bruised, to preach the acceptable year of the Lord."*

Jesus was unselfish, and we should follow His example. Lives were changed because of His willingness to help. Questions such as "What about me?" and "What's in it for me?" are inconsistent with true Christian character.

We can be compassionate. We must care what happens to others. We should be concerned about widows and orphans. Much of the emphasis concerning these issues is worldwide. Yet how often are we made aware of children in our local communities who need foster parenting or adoption? How many times have we been told about a widow in our local church in need?

All of us have the capacity to care, share, and make a difference. The number of people helped or money raised does not always measure difference making in God's eyes. God looks at the effort and the spirit we exhibit while helping others in need. Sometimes all that is needed is taking your meager resources and presenting them to God. This is clearly demonstrated in John 6:9. A young boy's lunch, consisting of five barley loaves and two fish, was used to feed a multitude. Five thousand men plus women and children were fed as a

result of his unselfishness.
"Make a Difference" Tyrone Keith Carroll Sr. Union Gospel Press Division

Ultimately, we should be determined to make a difference. We should never position ourselves to hear the following words from God:

> *For I was an hungered, and ye gave me no meat: I was thirsty, and ye gave me no drink: I was a stranger, and ye took me not in: naked, and ye clothed me not: sick and in prison, and ye visited me not. Matthew 25:42-43*

CHAPTER FOURTEEN

THE CALLED

"The process of connecting with and engaging others is filled with nuances and subtleties. We need to know who we are, what we are "called" to be and do, and what we bring to the table." Jack Dunigan

David was called (anointed to be a leader, King of Israel). As he labored daily in the field with his sheep, he was unknowingly undergoing the bitting process. Isolated from other family members, enduring and performing a task that none of his other siblings wanted, David fed the sheep, protected them, and guided them.

"Like pieces in a jigsaw puzzle, there is a place to fit, a void that is shaped just like who you are. Fortunate is the person who finds it. Frustrated are those who almost but not quite ever discover it." Jack Dunigan

Calling is by no means limited to a religious or spiritual experience. In more rigid societies, a person's calling was pre-determined by status and vocation. If your father was a tradesman, you were expected to be one too. However, today's culture is less rigid, especially in America where a person's birth does not pre-determine their destiny. "Calling is the means and passion that drives and fulfills. It is the ease with which our innate gifts and talents find expression and response. Calling is the higher purpose that drives us, that forms our core values and beliefs and that persuades us that effort is worth it and obstacles are worthy of the cunning it will take to overcome them. Calling means that we do nothing for very long for only the money. (However, money is very important. King Solomon wrote, *"Money answereth all things."*) We make a living by earning money, but we make a life by responding to and remaining faithful to our calling. Calling is a pursuit of values higher than money. Those who pursue their calling can give 100% to the job not because they are paid for their labor, but because they have found their place. They fit. Everything about them connects with the opportunity before them. Calling means that we do nothing for any amount of time that runs counter to our core purpose. Leaders who live by and for their calling never settle into a job because it pays the bills."

Dr. Gene Gatty, Bible Leadership Strategies for Living Life to Its Fullest, Bibleleadership.com

Nothing that changes this lost world and drives back Satan's forces is easy. If God has called you to pastor, then pastor. If God has called you to teach, then teach. If He has given you to be an Apostle, then be an Apostle. If you have been called to the office of a Prophet, then prophesy the true oracles of God. If God has called you as an evangelist, then evangelize. Whatever work God has called you to, make your call and election sure by holding onto the bit.

Finding Your Calling

James T. Wood, contributing writer of the Union Gospel Press, said that he heard in seminary, "It is easier to train the called than to call the trained." That means that without a calling, no amount of training will produce one's calling. Trying to manufacture a calling through schooling or working at a job will not create something that was never there. Callings are, as Frederick Buechner said, "where your deep gladness and the world's deep hunger meet" (*Wishful Thinking: A Theological ABC,* Harper & Row).

Before you can find your calling, you need to get rid of some misconceptions about calling. First, callings are not just for a few people. In the book of Ephesians, the Apostle Paul told the church that Christ had given gifts to the church in the form of apostles, prophets evangelists, pastors, and teachers (4:11) We often think of those functions in ministry as the ones to which people have been called, but that is not all Paul had to say. He went on to say that the purpose of those gifts (endowed to all the leaders in the church) is to equip and prepare all Christians for their own ministries. (vs. 12) Just because only a few are leaders in the church does not mean that only a few are called to ministry. We all are called to ministry; the leaders are called to equip us for our calling.

The second misconception about calling is that there are only a few types. This goes along with the misunderstanding that only the leaders in the church are called. The types of calling that God gives to His children are as varied as God's children. Again in Ephesians, Paul told the church that every single person is God's workmanship called for a purpose. (2:10) The word "workmanship" has the connotation of a masterpiece created by a master craftsman. You and I are unique, masterfully crafted creations of God. We were created not just to show off God's ability but for specific good works that "God hath before ordained." God made you uniquely, specifically, and masterfully for specific good works that only you can do. You were called by God because you were made by God, and He has made you with a purpose.

The final misconception about callings is that our callings will always look the same throughout our lives. We may be called to one type of ministry now; but as God continues to shape us, we may become better suited to a different type of ministry. Our life stages, our experiences, our passions, our fears, our talents, and our spiritual gifts all work together to affect our calling, and most of those things can change over time.

Everyone has a calling, not just a few leaders in the church. Every calling is as unique as the person called. Callings change over time as people change. So, then, how can you know your calling if you are not one of the few who receive it in a message from God?

First, you must serve. Every believer is created and called to do good works. (Eph. 2:10) Help those in need. Serve the least in the kingdom. You may not always like the work that you do, but exploring and learning about all the different types of service will help you discover, not only the ones you do not like, but also the ones that ignite the passion God has placed within you.

As you serve your church, your neighborhood, and your world, let leaders train and equip you. God has given the leaders to the church for that very purpose (Eph. 4:11-12) so let them equip you. Ask for help. Find a mentor. Learn something new. You might be surprised when you ask one of the leaders in your church to mentor you. It is likely that they do not get many requests like that. Too many people are content to let the leaders lead without taking the intentional steps to follow. Whatever your calling is, it is most certainly you are not called to inaction. God has called you to do something and you will never discover His calling if you are inactive.

As you serve and are mentored, learn about yourself. Your calling is an outgrowth of everything that God has done and is doing to shape you as a person. The more you know about yourself, the better you will know your calling.

Learn your personality. How do you approach people? How do you approach tasks? What gives you energy? What drains your energy? Learn your passions. What tragedies in the world make you angry? What triumphs in the world bring you the most joy? If you could change one thing in the world, what would it be?

Embrace your past. All the experiences that you have had in your life, both good and bad, have prepared you for God's calling. If you have suffered loss, you have a perspective on the loss that others do not have. Every obstacle that you have overcome is an obstacle that you can help others overcome as well.

Rely on the Spirit. God has given each Christian His Holy Spirit, not only as a guarantee of salvation (Eph. 1:14), but also as the source of gifts that empowers each to live out the calling of God in his life (Rom. 12:6-8; 1 Cor. 12:8-11; Gal. 5:22-23).

Finally, remember that your calling, the good works that God created you to do and the ministry that you are being equipped to carry out, does not exist only within the walls of the church building. Your calling may be to paid service at a church outside of your reformation, or it may be to serve God in a hospital or by driving a bus. God has called us to be in the world (John 17:15), living our lives as lights to everyone who sees us. We are not of the world, so we do not live according to its standards (Rom. 12:1-2), but we do live, work, play, and serve in the world.

When Jesus spoke about Judgment Day, He did not say that those who preached the best sermons would go to heaven or that those who wrote the best Bible commentaries would be with Him in the afterlife. Jesus said that those who serve others, *"come, ye blessed of my Father, inherit the kingdom prepared for you from the foundation of the world."* (Matt. 25:34) James T. Wood, Union Gospel Press, Summer Quarter (2017)

CHAPTER FIFTEEN

HUMILITY

Jesus made humility a virtue by His complete reversal of human values. It is the meek, not the mighty, who will be victorious. (Matthew 5:5) *"And whosoever shall exalt himself shall be abased; and he that shall humble himself shall be exalted."* (Matthew 23:12) The fact that we do not live humbly with one another is one reason why we often fail in our fight against Satan. The other reason is that we fail to humble ourselves before God and His Word.

> *These six things doth the LORD hate; yea, seven are an abomination unto him: 17) A proud look, a lying tongue, and hands that shed innocent blood, 18) An heart that deviseth wicked imaginations, feet that be swift in*

> *running to mischief, 19) A false witness that speaketh lies, and he that soweth discord among brethren.*
> Proverbs 6:16-19

We are to show love toward one another and respect one another's gifts. In the house of God there is no room for jealousy and strife. This is not accomplished in and of ourselves alone. We need the guidance and working of the Holy Spirit who brings about maturity through the process of spiritual bitting that is necessary to perfect the love, honor and respect we should have one towards another. There is turmoil within church congregations. Leaders who exhibit arrogance often produce arrogant followers. The quality of humility has to do with how we regard ourselves relative to how we regard others. Peter writes. *"All of you be subject one to another, and be clothed with humility."* The "clothing of humility" will not look fashionable according to this world's standard of fashion. It would most likely look like the coveralls our forefathers wore in the cotton and tobacco fields. It would be the boots and gloves of the worker who labors diligently to keep the church looking decent and in order. In the church, "clothing of humility" may be the usher's badge or the mother's apron. It would apply to the one who teaches the Sunday school class, or the one who labors in the kitchen cooking and overseeing collation for afternoon services, missionaries who take meals to a bereaved family.

Ah, to be more like Jesus! "So meek and lowly, so humble and holy."

Failing to humble ourselves in relationships is an indication of failure to humble ourselves before God. Jesus humbled himself took on flesh that He might condemn sin in the flesh. The world would have us buy into the saying "only the strong survive". But the Christian who has vowed to follow Christ knows that victory comes through submission. After all, our mission is not to survive, but to live! Jesus said, *"I came that you might have life and have it more abundantly."* Ah, to be more like Jesus! "So meek and lowly, so humble and holy." Only God will honor the humble. In Matthew 18:3, Jesus said, *"Except ye be converted, and become as little children, ye shall not enter into the kingdom of heaven."* The person who brings himself down to such an utterly dependent state is the one who will be greatest in the kingdom, because he has learned to be dependent on God's power and not on his own intelligence.

Experiencing the "new birth" does not instantly transform us into godly people. Godliness involves a lifelong process of growth. Therefore, Christians must never be content with the level of spiritual maturity they have attained. Any godly qualities gained must become greater.

> *...giving all diligence, add to your faith virtue; and to virtue knowledge; 6) And to knowledge temperance; and to temperance patience; and to patience godliness; 7) And to godliness brotherly kindness; and to brotherly kindness charity. 8) For if these things be in you, and abound, they make you that ye shall neither be barren nor unfruitful in the knowledge of our Lord Jesus Christ.*
> *II Peter 1:5-8*

Real humility is serving without regard for the praise or accolades of man

A Christian who does not actively pursue spiritual growth runs the risk of being cast out and trodden under foot of men. Humility is a virtue that many leaders have yet to attain. Some have mastered the "art" of leadership rather than the humbleness of servitude to a point where they are able to display false humility, insisting on having one's own way or thinking that they have all the answers, and insisting that they be given praise or preference is not humility. Real humility is serving without regard for the praise or accolades of man. It is no surprise that 1 John 2:16 places "the pride of life," the lust of the flesh, and the lust of the eyes on the same level as a deep-rooted central position of sin.

Humility Flows in Both Directions:

> *And behold, a woman in the city, which was a sinner, when she knew that Jesus sat at meat in the Pharisee's house, brought an alabaster box of ointment... And he turned to the woman, and said unto Simon, Seest thou this woman? I entered into thine house, thou gavest me no water for my feet: but she hath washed my feet with tears, and wiped them with the hairs of her head.*
> *Luke 7:37, 44*

It took as much humility for Jesus to permit a woman to wash His feet as it took Him to wash the disciple's feet.

> *He riseth from supper, and laid aside his garments; and took a towel, and girded himself." After that he poureth water into a basin, and began to wash the disciple's feet, and to wipe them with the towel wherewith he was girded.*
> *John 13:4-5*

Jesus taught a supreme example of humility of servant leadership to his disciples. If he as their Lord and Master was willing to do work of the lowest servant, then his disciples must be prepared to do the same. After the Lord's ascension they were to do greater works, they were (except Judas) to be leaders, fishers of men. But Jesus wanted them to know that they would fulfill those duties effectively only if they were willing to be servants. Those who endure the process of spiritual bitting emerge as willing workers. It is the belief of some that Judas Iscariot had left the room before Jesus had begun to wash feet and it is believed by others that he was still there. The Bible does not clearly state whether Judas Iscariot was present when Jesus washed the disciples' feet, but if he was, then Jesus also washed his feet. Jesus made no distinction; He humbly washed the feet of the one who would betray him.

> *Yea, mine own familiar friend in whom I trusted, which did eat of my bread, hath lifted up his heel against me.*
> *Psalm 41: 9*

Humility and the humbling of self are not popular traits in today's world and seems unappealing to most of us. Our perception on humility can be radically changed from a worldly prospective if we will ponder and meditate on the greatest example of humility in history -- Jesus Christ. Throughout his life on earth, Jesus demonstrated a spirit of profound humility, saying that he came *"not to be served, but to serve, and to give his life a ransom for many."* (Matt. 20:28) On his last night with the disciples, he took a towel and basin and washed their dirty feet, instructing them to follow his example of servanthood with one another.

In Jesus we have the example of all examples: those who humble themselves will be exalted! And this is meant to guide our lives in our Christian walk. If we humble ourselves, we can trust God to do diligence to exalt us. JESUS IS THE WAY, THE TRUTH AND HE IS LIFE!

The Joy of Serving Others:

To know what is right is commendable, but to actually do what is a right defeat Satan's destructive plans and gives fulfillment to the plan of God. When we serve others we forget about ourselves and only focus on the joy of serving others. A prideful attitude robs, kills, steals and destroys the giving of loving service to others. The spiritual bit produces defeat to that attitude and releases the joy in rendering service to others. Rather than talk of the "duty" of service; we should emphasize the "privilege" of imitating Christ in service.

> *Let this mind be in you, which was also in Christ Jesus:*
> *Phil. 2:5*

One ought not serve unless it is out of a genuine attitude of love and concern. However, on the other hand, if being served by someone else who is attempting to express a genuine attitude of love, respect and honor, it should graciously be accepted.

> *Then took Mary a pound of ointment of spikenard, very costly, and anointed the feet of Jesus, and wiped his feet with her hair: and the house was filled with the odour of the ointment.*
> *John 12:3*

Spiritual restraint guides into the highest level of humility – *"love your enemies, bless them that curse you, do good to them that hate you and pray for them which despitefully use you, and persecute you." "Love your neighbor as yourself!"* Love is as love does. God so loved!

Foot washing is only one example of humble servant leadership. If in any way we seek to put the needs of others ahead of our own, we are following the example of our Master Servant Leader, Jesus Christ.

> *And the servant of the Lord must not strive; but be gentle unto all men, apt to teach, patient, In meekness instructing those that oppose themselves.*
> *II Timothy 2:24-25a*

From Humbleness to Humility

There are many biblical examples of pride and its consequences in the lives of individuals, and they offer valuable lessons for us. A couple of notable examples are that of King Uzziah and King Saul.

King Uzziah became king of Judah at age sixteen and set his heart to seek God and put himself under the spiritual mentorship of Zechariah. The key to Uzziah's success was his desire to seek God. As long as he sought the Lord, God made him prosper. As a result, he acquired wealth and also became politically and militarily powerful. His leadership resulted in amazing successes; it was superb. His fame spread as far as the entrance of Egypt and his leadership strengths were envied by other kings. However, as his fame spread, things began to change. He grew proud which led to his destruction. As a result of his blessings, King Uzziah began to think more highly of himself than he ought. He developed an exaggerated sense of his own importance and abilities.

> *But when he was strong his heart was lifted up, to his destruction, for he transgressed against the Lord, his God by entering the temple of the Lord to burn incense on the altar of incense. 17) So Azariah the priest went in after him, and with him were eighty priests of the Lord... 18) And they withstood King Uzziah, and said to him, "It is not for you, Uzziah, to burn incense to the LORD, but for the priests, the sons of Aaron, who are consecrated to burn incense.*
>
> *Get out of the sanctuary, for you have trespassed! You shall have no honor from the LORD God." Then Uzziah became furious; and he had a censer in his hand to burn incense. And while he was angry with the priests, leprosy broke out on his forehead, before the priests in the house of the LORD, beside the incense altar. 20) And Azariah the chief priest and all the priests looked at*

> *him, and there, on his forehead, he was leprous; so they thrust him out of that place. Indeed, he also hurried to get out, because the LORD had struck him. 21) King Uzziah was a leper until the day of his death.*
> II Chronicles 26:16-21 NKJV

The pride of King Uzziah's heart brought very serious consequences upon him illustrating the biblical warnings that *"pride goeth before destruction."* (Prov. 16:18) His eulogy did not read of success, prosperity, military genius, or one who followed God's commands, it was short and humiliating: "He is a leper."

Saul was told to go and smite Amalek, and utterly destroy all that they had and spare them not. However, Saul spared the life of Agag the King of the Amalekites and the best of the livestock to offer sacrifice unto the LORD. Therefore, God ripped King Saul's kingdom from him and gave it to David.

> *And Samuel said, Hath the LORD as great delight in burnt-offerings and sacrifices, as in obeying the voice of the LORD? Behold, to obey is better than sacrifice, and to hearken than the fat of rams. For rebellion is as the sin of witchcraft, and stubbornness is as iniquity and idolatry. Because thou hast rejected the word of the LORD, he hath also rejected thee from being King.*
> I Samuel 15:22-23

Just as the disciples who followed Jesus were concerned about who would be the greatest in the kingdom, sadly enough the attitude of self-promotion, pursuit of reputation, influence, and success is evident in some ministry leaders today. If the apostles had to struggle with it, Christians today should not think themselves exempt. Take not the bit out of the horse's mouth!

The Root of Pride Goes Deep Into The Soul

Just as the root of a dandelion flower, the root of pride goes deep into the soul. It's seeds lodge in the tiniest encouraging cracks. The danger of pride is that it feeds and flourishes on the blessings of God. Spiritual pride is very dangerous and when people in leadership are corrupted by it, they can produce widespread suffering throughout the church.

Pride can be obvious or carefully concealed.

Pride can be summarized as an attitude of self-sufficiency, self-importance, and self-exaltation in relation to God. Toward others, it is an attitude of contempt and indifference. Thomas A. Tarrants III, D. Min. Vice President of Ministry, C.S. Lewis Institute observed that, "Pride is spiritual cancer: it eats up the very possibility of love, or contentment, or even common sense." The depth of pride can vary from person to person. It can be obvious or carefully concealed.

It was pride, not humility that caused Lucifer to be cast out of heaven and Adam and Eve to be cast out of Eden. When the Bridegroom comes, have your lamp of humility trimmed and burning bright. Don't get left behind!

The Formation of a Pearl

The birth of a pearl is truly a miraculous event. Unlike gemstones of precious metals that must be mined from the earth, pearls are grown by live oysters far below the surface of the sea. Gemstones must be cut and polished to bring out their beauty. But pearls need no such treatment to reveal their loveliness. They are born from oysters complete with a shimmering iridescence, luster and soft inner glow unlike any other gem on earth.

A natural pearl begins its life as a foreign object such as a parasite or piece of shell that accidentally lodges itself in an oyster's body. The oyster begins to secrete a smooth hard crystalline substance around the irritant in order to protect itself. This is called "nacre." As long as the irritant remains within its body, the oyster will be completely encased by the silky crystalline coatings. And the result, ultimately, is the lovely and lustrous gem called a pearl.

How something so wondrous emerges from an oyster's way of protecting itself is one of nature's loveliest surprises. For the nacre is not just a soothing substance, it is composed of microscopic crystals of calcium carbonate, aligned perfectly with one another, so that light passing along the axis of one crystal is reflected and refracted by another to produce a rainbow of light and color.

Cultured pearls share the same properties as natural pearls. Oysters form cultured pearls in an almost identical fashion. The only difference is a person carefully implants the irritant in the oyster, rather than leaving it to chance. They then step aside and let nature create its miracle.
American Pearl Inc., www.amricanparl.com

A little irritation over time creates pure hearts

For one to walk in humility, gentleness, patience and love, the irritant (spiritual bit) lodges in the heart, not by chance, but by the power of the Holy Spirit; the servant leader is the cultured pearl that is formed over time whose beauty is manifested within the body of Christ. Cultured, not natural, because humankind is not naturally humble, gentle, patient or loving. Humankind becomes cultured if there is submission to the controlled spiritual bitting of the Holy Spirit. A little irritation over time creates pure hearts that can be transformed into walking in love, joy, peace longsuffering, gentleness, goodness, and faith, otherwise known as the fruit of the spirit.

Pride and Humility

Pride is a great sin. It is the devil's most effective and destructive tool. Pride and arrogance seem to be more prevalent among the rich and famous. Unfortunately, it is also found in some religious leaders and can be discerned in ordinary people as well. Yet there are some who have come to realize how dangerous it is to our souls and how greatly it hinders our intimacy with God and love for others. Humility, according to worldly standards is seen as weakness and therefore few know much about it or pursue it. For the good of our souls, then, we need to gain a clearer understanding of pride and humility and how to forsake the one and embrace the other.

Pride Goes Before Destruction

Pride first appears in the Bible in Genesis the third chapter where we see the devil, that "proud spirit," using pride as the avenue by which to seduce our first parents. Taking the form of a serpent, his approach was simple yet deadly. First, he arrogantly contradicted what God had said to Adam about eating the forbidden fruit and consequently charged God with lying. This shocking rejection of God's word caused Eve to plunge into unbelief and aroused doubt in her mind about the truthfulness and reliability of God. In the next breath, the devil drew her into deeper deception by contending that God's reason for lying was to keep her from enjoying all the possibilities inherent in being Godlike. This clever plot was aimed at undermining her confidence in the goodness and love of God and arousing the desire to become as God.
The desire to lift up and exalt ourselves beyond our place as God's creature lies at the heart of pride. As Eve in her

now confused and deceived state of mind considered the possibilities, her desire to become Godlike grew stronger. She began to look at the forbidden fruit in a new light, as something attractive to the eyes and pleasant to the touch. Desire increased, giving rise to rationalization and a corresponding erosion of the will to resist and say no. Pride is a classic case of unbridled lust of the flesh!

Finally, weakened by unbelief, enticed by pride, and ensnared by self-deception, she opted for autonomy and disobeyed God's command. In just a few deft moves, the devil was able to use pride to bring about Eve's downfall and plunge the human race into spiritual ruin. This ancient but all-too-familiar process confronts each of us daily.

> *Each person is tempted when he is lured and enticed by his own desire. Then desire, when it is conceived gives birth to sin, and sin when it is fully grown brings forth death.*
> *James 1: 14-15*

Because it is Satan's most dangerous subtle tool, and exist unrecognized to self, we must earnestly seek God in prayer and ask him to reveal to us any sinful pride in our lives so we can repent and forsake it. The prideful spirit is of the devil. He is slothful, sneaky and conniving. He implants and lies dormant for a season. Then at a most inopportune time for the victim, but opportune for him he rears his demonic head.

Aside from pride that is sin, there is a good type of pride. Paul was proud of the churches he had established. But this was not arrogant or self-exalting pride. He made it clear that his accomplishments were the fruit of God's grace to him and through him. Occasionally Paul mentions boasting, but this is a matter of highlighting what God has done by his grace, either through Paul or in those in the churches. It is never self-exalting. These days most of us will say that we are proud of our children or our favorite sports team or perhaps something we have accomplished. In cases like this, one hopes that saying "I am proud of ... thanks be to God, or to God be the glory."

God takes pleasure in our efforts to humble ourselves

Pride is a universal human problem. Everyone suffers from it to some degree. When we have exalted ourselves in pride. God does not want to punish us and bring us low but rather to forgive and restore us. He says again and again in scripture, humble yourselves, and I will exalt you. This gives us hope and encouragement. God takes pleasure in our efforts to humble ourselves, and he loves to bless and exalt the humble.

Admire and Seek The Humility of Christ

How do we gain the mind of Christ and humble ourselves? To put on the mind of Christ, we must want to make a conscious effort to ponder, understand, and adopt Jesus' way of thinking, his values and attitudes to become ours. His strong emphasis on humility and meekness and his examples of it must take hold of our thinking, our desires and our conduct. We must admire his humility and want it for ourselves. For this to happen, we need to earnestly and regularly pray for the Holy Spirit to change our hearts, for it is impossible to do it in our own strength. The process of spiritual bitting perfects the spirit of meekness and humility.

True humility is our greatest friend

Humility is having a right view of self in relation to God and others and acting accordingly. *"What doth the LORD require of thee, but to do justly, and to love mercy and to walk humbly with thy God."* (Micah 6:8) If we were to consider ourselves relative to who God is we would conclude among other thing that we are God's creatures: small, finite, dependent, limited in intelligence and ability, prone to sin, and soon to die and face God's judgment. But we are also God's children: created, loved, and redeemed by God's grace alone, not by anything in or of ourselves; and gifted by God with certain unique gifts, abilities, resources, and advantages, which are to be used for His glory.

Having a right view of God and self has a profound effect on our relationships with others. As Paul goes on to say in Romans, *"Live in harmony with one another. Do not be haughty, but associate with the lowly."* (Romans 12:16) And as he said to the Philippians, *"Let nothing be done through strife or vainglory; but in lowliness of mind let each esteem other better than themselves. Look not every man on his own things, but every man also on the things of others"* (Phil 2:3-4) As we refuse to be preoccupied with self and our own importance and seek to love and serve others, it will reorient us from self-centeredness to other-centeredness to serve and care for others just as Jesus did for us.

True humility is our greatest friend. It increases our hunger for God's word and opens our hearts to his Spirit. It leads to intimacy with God, who knows the proud from afar, but dwells with him who is of a contrite and lowly spirit. It imparts the aroma of Christ to all whom we encounter. It is a sign of greatness in the kingdom of God.

> *...I dwell in the high and holy place, with him also that is of a contrite and humble spirit, to revive the spirit of the humble, and to revive the heart of the contrite one.*
> Isaiah 57:15

Developing the identity, attitude, and conduct of a humble servant does not happen overnight. Thomas A. Tarrants, III, Vice President of Ministry, C. S. Lewis Institute compares it to peeling an onion: you cut away one layer only to find another beneath it. But it does happen. As we forsake pride and seek to humble ourselves by a daily and deliberate choice to depend on the Holy Spirit, humility grows in our souls.

Forsake Not The Spiritual Bit

Humbleness is not weakness; it is strength that is under control. It takes great strength to maintain self-control in the face of adversity. The fact is that until a person's heart is humbled they can never receive the grace of God, which is a gift that He only gives to those who are of a humble and contrite spirit.

The heart that is humble is open to receive. Children are naturally humble, and therefore it is no wonder that Jesus used them to teach a lesson on humility. Jesus is not saying that we are to be childish but childlike, eager and open to receive. There is a huge difference. True humility is thinking more highly of others than self and putting the interests of others ahead of your own. Jesus humbled himself and took on flesh that He might condemn sin in the flesh. He was thinking of us!

God Exalts The Humble

King Josiah's heart was willing to obey God. The king tore his clothes and wept before God. This contrite act revealed the king's humble heart and God heard his prayers.

> *Because thine heart was tender and thou didst humble thyself before God when thou heardest his words against this place, and against the inhabitants thereof, and humbledest thyself before me, and didst rend thy clothes, and weep before me; I have even heard thee, also saith the Lord.*
> *II Chronicles 34:27*

A tender, humble heart is one that is receptive to change and one that is open to being in submission to God. King David wrote:

> *The sacrifices of God are a broken spirit; a broken and a contrite heart, O God, thou wilt not despise.*
> *Psalm 51:17*

If a person exalts himself, they will be humbled, but if they humble themselves, God will exalt them because God exalts the humble and humbles the exalted.

> *Neither be ye called masters, for one is your master, even Christ. But he that is greatest among you shall be your servant. And whoever shall exalt himself shall be abased; and he that shall humbles himself shall be exalted.*
> *Matthew 23:10-12*

James wrote *"Humble yourselves before the Lord, and he will exalt you."* It is better to humble ourselves than to have God do it for us. Advice to those in church ministry today who seek to be the greatest: be the servant. Jesus came to serve not be served.

Paul encouraged the church of Ephesus to *"walk in a manner worthy of the calling to which you have been called, with all lowliness and meekness, with longsuffering forbearing one another in love, endeavoring to keep the unity of the Spirit in the bond of peace." Ephesians 4:1-3*

The manner in which we walk should be worthy of our calling. To walk with *"all lowliness and meekness, with longsuffering, forbearing one another in love"* is worthy.

SECTION FOUR

CHAPTER SIXTEEN

THE ANOINTING

The anointing is a gift that functions easily when it is moving. You cannot turn it on and you cannot turn it off. The Holy Spirit, the giver of the anointing is completely in control. In his book, "The Anointing Yesterday, Today and Tomorrow" R. T. Kendall evokes thought that I have laid out in this section so that it brings to light a greater understanding of the word "anointing". What many of us see on any given Sunday is what I will term as the "been through the fire anointing, or been through the flood anointing" aka "been through the bitting process." Kendall takes us through the various aspects and stigmas of anointing. He encourages leaders to move outside their comfort zone. He embraces thoughts on today's leaders versus tomorrow's leaders. He explores the secret anointing. He cautions about being held hostage by yesterday's anointing. He warns about not being open to how God is moving today and that the Holy Spirit may not necessarily manifest His anointing in the same manner tomorrow. Every generation has to discover the direction our sovereign God is moving and move in that direction. This section contains excerpts from Kendall's book and embraces such topics as:

The Stigma of the Anointing - The Greek word for stigma is 'Stizo' meaning to prick, tattoo, and mark as with a sharp instrument. Stigma synonymous with the word skandalon means offense. The preached word at times can become an offense when it is not what folk want to hear.

The Loneliness of the Anointing - Today's Apostles, Pastors, Evangelists, Prophets, Teachers or anyone committed to kingdom work often walk alone as did Samuel, Moses, Abraham, Elijah and Paul. In addition to the stigma of loneliness there is the stigma of being misunderstood. In order to accomplish God's will, there will be times when you cannot explain why you are doing what you do. Our sovereign God tells or shows us as we move forward on a need to know basis. As Noah, we simply trust Him and follow His lead. You may have to separate yourself from the crowd or you will be separated by the Holy Spirit as Paul and Barnabas were. Certain relationships will have to be put aside for the sake of God's will just as Paul had to put aside his relationship with Barnabas because of Mark.

Yesterday's servant leader - is a person who ceases to be relevant in the ways of God's current movement. He or she may continue to minister, but such a person has lost it; they are out of touch. They are saying the same thing said in previous years when it probably had some spiritual significance, but carries no weight for the present day generation.

Today's servant leader - has to muster up the degree of courage required to perform the right now tasks at hand. Samuel had to break with his comfort zone regime. He was highly trained in hearing God's voice and had to decide whether he wanted to continue to hear and be God's today anointed man or mourn for Saul and become like Saul - God's yesterday man. In other words, Samuel knew he could either mourn for Saul and break with God; or obey God and break with Saul. Samuel chose to obey God. All relationships must be subservient to a relationship with God.

CHAPTER SEVENTEEN

THE SECRET ANOINTING

Just as God did for David, He has a way of finding us when His time for us comes. After He secretly anoints us, He has to prepare and refine us. There are two kinds of preparation: Academic and Spiritual. Academic is important but not the most important. Then there is the refinement that is often brought about by suffering. Suffering was David's credential to a greater anointing. To use a thought by T.D. Jakes, Saul was David's "sparring partner." Many times the best way to get closer to God in your anointing is for God to give you a powerful enemy who is consumed with hatred for you. This teaches you to know what it takes to become more like Jesus--meek and lowly, humble and holy.

Camouflage

David's secret anointing was camouflaged by certain gifts and talents. David was blessed to be a musician as well as an outdoorsman of bravery. These gifts and talents would put him in good standing with Saul.

> *The Spirit of the LORD departed from Saul, and an evil spirit from the LORD troubled him. Then answered one of the servants and said, Behold, I have seen a son of Jesse the Bethlehemite, that is cunning in playing, a mighty valiant man, and a man of war, and prudent in matters, and a comely person, and the LORD is with him.*
> *I Sam 16:14,18*

This was David's first opportunity to perform in the royal palace. Whenever David played before Saul, the evil spirit would leave him. David's next opportunity was to demonstrate his warrior talent.

> *And the Philistine said, I defy the armies of Israel this day; give me a man that we may fight together. When Saul and all Israel heard those words of the Philistine, they were dismayed, and greatly afraid. And David said to Saul, Let no man's heart fail because of him; thy servant will go and fight with this Philistine.*
> *I Sam. 17:10-11;32*

Spiritual Discernment

David's secret anointing coupled with his warrior gift, enabled him to see Israel's enemy for what and who he was before an Omnipotent God. God gives spiritual discernment to enhance your secret anointing. With it, you are able to 'size up' your enemy from afar and be equipped to make right decisions at the right time. Remember, your enemy, the devil is a trickster, and a deceiver. In David's case, Goliath was to the natural eyes of Saul, a huge dreadful giant, but David was given a spiritual discernment that allowed him to see Goliath for who he really was—"an uncircumcised Philistine."

With spiritual discernment, spiritual cataracts are removed to enable you to see what the natural eye cannot see. Timid tongues are given boldness to say what others are afraid to say. The anointing begins to be a "stizo."

Ability and Limitations

David put on Saul's armor and found that it was not comfortable. He had to test his anointing in his own garment – the garment of faith. David's faith was not in Saul, nor was it in Saul's garment – but in the living God of Israel.

David's secret anointing combined with his natural gift won the day. He continued to grow from strength to strength. However, he began to get too much praise. The women chanted, "Saul has slain his thousands, and David his tens of thousands." Too much praise can become a heavy helmet. Although David wanted to remain loyal to Saul, the feeling was not mutual. Often those at the helm cannot handle too much praise being given to those who sit under them. Jealousy ensues and a breach in the relationship occurs. If there is ever a time to let God fight your battle, it is certainly now. Fighting the battle of envy and jealousy from a once friend and confidant is far worse than fighting your known enemy.

Refinement and Preparation

There is a purpose for refinement and preparation. God had a different idea for David; Saul was to be the means of David's sanctification. David wasn't ready to be king. Yes, he had a powerful anointing, but he needed to be honed and refined. In the years to come, the anointing in David was to increase and develop so that when his time truly came, David would be a servant transformed by the Holy Spirit.

A man or woman with a secret anointing always needs further preparation. You do not get the necessary refinement by merely praying for more of the Holy Spirit. Jesus had all the Holy Spirit that there was—the Spirit without limit. (John 3:34) *"Yet, although He was a son, He learned obedience from what He suffered."* (Heb.5:8)

Passport To Greater Anointing

Suffering was David's passport to a greater anointing. Though the Spirit came upon him in power, he needed Saul as insurance for yet more power. David also needed a friend. He found that in Saul's son Jonathan. A friend is someone who knows all about you and still likes you. Your secret anointing will not only need refining but also a friendship that compensates for the suffering. A true friend will tell you the truth. Some people only want friends who tell them what they want to hear. Therein lies danger.

God doesn't need a Saul to refine His servants, but He uses them to mold His chosen. The challenge of having a secret anointing is that you may have to wait a long time for your time to come. Many fall by the wayside because they cannot wait. It was nearly twenty years between David's secret anointing and his public anointing, but he knew how to wait. He waited patiently, not grudgingly. He waited with respect for the one currently holding the position. Eventually he was given a platform. He became the greatest king Israel ever had. David penned in Psalm 27:14 *"Wait on the LORD and be of good courage..."* surely David knew about waiting!

The secret anointing in you, though you are not high profile, will still be a threat to the enemy God chooses for your refinement. Just as David could not hide his secret anointing, you will not be able to hide your secret anointing. Though it be secret, it will shine through, so will the envy and jealousy against you - as a thorn in your side. But, God's Grace is sufficient!

CHAPTER EIGHTEEN

MOVING OUTSIDE YOUR COMFORT ZONE

Comfort Zone: A situation in which you feel comfortable and in which your ability and determination are not being tested. [Cambridge Dictionary]

[Wikipedia] A comfort zone is a psychological state in which things feel familiar to a person and they are at ease and in control of their environment, experiencing low levels of anxiety and stress. In this zone, a steady level of performance is possible. Bardwick defines the term as a "behavioral state where a person operates in an anxiety-neutral

position." Brown describes it as "where our uncertainty, scarcity and vulnerability are minimized, where we believe we'll have access to enough - to enough love, food, talent, time, admiration. Where we feel we have some control."
Judith M. Bardwick, (1995) Danger in the Comfort Zone
Brene Brown (2012) "Daring Greatly" – How the Courage to be Vulnerable Transforms The Way We Live, Love, Parent, and Lead

Samuel's Comfort Zone

Samuel was the son of Elkanah and Hannah. Before he was born, Hannah made a vow unto the LORD, *"O LORD of hosts, if thou wilt indeed look on the affliction of thine handmaid, and remember me, and not forget thine handmaid, but wilt give unto thine handmaid a man child, then I will give him unto the LORD all the days of his life, and there shall no razor come upon his head."* (I Samuel 1:11) After Samuel's birth, his mother took him to Eli the priest to be lent to the LORD all of his days. Samuel ministered unto the LORD under the guidance of Eli. When Eli died, Samuel stepped comfortably into his role as judge and priest of Israel. Samuel became more and more recognized throughout all of Israel. He anointed Israel's first king (Saul), and his successor (David). The LORD did not let one word of Samuel "fall to the ground." Everyone knew that Samuel was established to be a prophet of the LORD. (I Samuel 3:19)

Moving Outside Your Comfort Zone

Moving out of your comfort zone is never easy especially when it bares a word of judgment. Samuel's first encounter to move out of his comfort zone was when the LORD told him concerning the judgment He was going to perform against Eli's house. When confronted with the decision to tell or not to tell Eli, Samuel chose to tell.

Comfort zones become the proverbial comfort blanket

When Saul became rejected by the LORD, Samuel was once more ordered to move outside his comfort zone. *"And the LORD said unto Samuel, How long wilt thou mourn for Saul, seeing I have rejected him from reigning over Israel? Fill thine horn with oil, and go. I will send thee to Jesse the Bethlehemite: for I have provided me a king among his sons."* (I Samuel 16:1) Stepping out of your comfort zone can raise anxiety and generate a stress response. Samuel's stress response was to mourn for Saul's rejection.

Comfort zones become the proverbial comfort blanket. You feel you need it in order to function. When you are forced to move outside of your comfort zone, you may feel threatened and vulnerable.

Samuel felt threaten. Before going to anoint the next king he asked the LORD, *"How can I go? If Saul hear it, he will kill me. And the LORD said, Take an heifer with thee, and say, I am come to sacrifice to the LORD."* (I Samuel 16:2)

Moving Out As It Applies To Relationships

Samuel had enjoyed a relationship with Saul that had to be broken because he valued his relationship with God as greater. He was highly trained in hearing God's voice and had to decide whether he wanted to continue to hear and be God's anointed man for today or comfortably continue to mourn for Saul and become like Saul, God's yesterday man. No friendship or relationship is worth its weight in gold if it does not have an inflexible commitment to God's glory first. Today's man or woman must be committed to maintaining a relationship with God and be willing if necessary to break off any secondary relationships. This may be awkward, it may be painful, but no relationship with any person should surpass our relationship with God.

Moving Out as It Applies To The Word and The Holy Spirit

Some of us may find it easier to be open to the Word than to the Holy Spirit. We feel safe with the Word, but fearful that the Holy Spirit may lead us out of our comfort zone. The Holy Spirit is the author of the Word and He will not lead us in any way that is contrary to what He has written through His sovereign instrument, the Bible. In the words of Bishop Leroy C. E. Newman, Chief Apostle of the Friendly Church of the Apostolic Faith, and the General Overseer of Friendly Church Ministries International, "God will never take you to a place in ministry where you are forced to retreat."

Newman, Bishop Leroy C.E., and Pastor Israel E. Newman (2015), *The Pursuit of Excellence-Developing Your Personal Ministry "New Enlightenments"*

When you are in your comfort zone you are in your secure element; outside of it you may initially feel like a fish out of water.

P.U.S.H. Out

P. - Pray
U. - Until
S. - Something
H. - Happens

That something will become your next comfort zone, your next fulfillment, your greater anointing!

CHAPTER NINETEEN

TODAY'S SERVANT LEADER

The preached word is not always received with joy. Sometimes it becomes an offense when it is not what folk want to hear or when it is given in a manner people are not familiar. The word will either be accepted or rejected. Therefore, today's man or woman servant leader must have the boldness and fortitude to bear the pain of loneliness, the stigma of being misunderstood, the perplexity of lost relationships, and the suffering of rejection. Today's man or woman servant leader must stand as a warrior at all times. Paul told the Ephesians to *"Put on the whole armor of God, that ye may be able to stand against the wiles of the devil."* (Eph. 6:11)

Bearing the Pain of Loneliness

Jay E. Adams counsels that there is no choice between pain and no pain; in this life we have no such choice. Rather, choices lie in the areas of (1) how are pain and suffering viewed and (2) how are pain and suffering used. The cross dignified suffering by giving it meaning and demonstrated that it can have far-reaching effects of good.

Adams, Jay E. (1979), A Theology of Christian Counseling, "Counseling and Suffering"

These days, collective leadership is the "thing"

There will be times when Today's man or woman servant leader will have to break with the crowd to fulfill God's purpose. Loneliness goes with the call of being today's man or woman. These days, collective leadership is the "thing". The greater the consensus, the lighter the stigma; no individual accountability, the buck can be passed around to be shared.

Stigma of Being Misunderstood

The paramount stigma of being today's man or woman servant leader is that of being misunderstood. Nothing is more painful than being misunderstood by those most close to you. You may have a gift of great discernment, or a sense of great supremacy on your life and not be able to explain or convince family members or other close friends that what you are feeling is a calling of God unless the Holy Spirit shows them as well.

The offense in some people's anointing is camouflaged by God's setup. Joseph's brothers even his father could not have felt more justified in their disgust for Joseph's dreams. God's setup is to be on the lookout for tomorrow's man or woman servant. Joseph was setup to be God's tomorrow man in position to feed His people in times of famine. Be not discouraged when men don't understand your anointing. You are being setup to feed in times of spiritual famine.

Rejection

It's hard not to take rejection personally, especially if you have been close to the people who can't go along with you. However, when you know you are carrying out God's mandate, you have to take a stand that withstands the most vehement criticism.

It has been said that the greatest opposition to what God is doing today comes from those who were on the cutting edge of what God was doing yesterday, that the greatest hostility to what God is doing now comes from those who were on the front line of what God was doing yesterday. The greatest attacks on any current move of the Holy Spirit often comes from those who were part of yesterday's move of the Spirit – Jealousy being the reason.

Perplexity of Rejection

The perplexity of rejection is that sometimes wounds from a trusted friend can bite or hurt and this has nothing to do with the spiritual bitting. Truth is, we all need someone around us who will not be rubber stamps and who will warn and rebuke when necessary. Those who become un-teachable and unaccountable because they have achieved a measure of success will find themselves rejected by God's today's anointing with no possibility of becoming tomorrow's man or woman servant leaders.

The Suffering of Lost Relationships

Don't risk being accepted by people but rejected by God because of sin. Dr. Listra Lawrence's mantra is "If you can master [sin] privately, you can master publicly."
Lawrence, Dr. Listra, Instructor, Berean Bible Institute & School of Ministry

No friendship or relationship is worth its weight in goal if it does not have an inflexible commitment to God's glory first. Samuel had to break with Saul. Today's man or woman servant leaders often find themselves in the awkward position of breaking away from relationships. Sentimental attachments must be put aside. Nostalgia has to go. Precious memories no matter how they linger are never sufficient to keep a relationship in tact if all parties are not committed to hearing God's voice.

The truth is hard for most people to take

The more Jesus taught about the spiritual nature of his kingdom and his Messiah-ship, the more people became disillusioned and disenchanted. They realized that Jesus was not the kind of king they thought he would be--and not the kind of king they wanted. They didn't abandon Jesus because he wasn't a good marketing strategist or a good salesman. They didn't abandon Jesus because there was anything wrong with his message. They abandoned him because the truth is hard for most people to take.
Youssef, Michael, (2013), The Leadership Style of Jesus, "Guidelines for Lonely Leaders"

No covenant with any person, church, group or organization should be based on sheer human loyalty to one another. Today's man or woman servant leader must get his or her priority straight and that priority is maintaining a "today" relationship with God.

CHAPTER TWENTY

TOMORROW'S SERVANT LEADERS

Tomorrow's servant of Christ is typified by David. He had the anointing without the crown. Having the anointing but not the platform can be very painful. Waiting for the platform can be long and arduous but worth the wait. David became Israel's greatest king. He emerged from being Secretly Anointed to being Today's Man and for the next 39 years, Tomorrow's Man, publicly ruling the United Kingdom of Israel.

Unconscious Preparation

For David there was an unconscious preparation in his

own household, *"A man's enemies will be the members of his own household."* (Matt. 10:36) But God saw in David what Jesse underestimated – a young man with a heart after God. The feeling that we never come up to standard can be frustrating. God will refine you so that when your time comes you will be ready and trustworthy of a greater anointing. Your refining platform may be obscure away from the high profile platforms, usually one that no one else wants. It will not be a glamorous platform, but designed by God. For David it was on the backside of the mountain. Wherever your refining platform may be, serve in it unto the Glory of God! You will not emerge perfect, but you will be ready. "You are a trophy of his kindness, a partaker of his mission. Not perfect by any means but closer to perfection than you've ever been. Steadily stronger, gradually better, certainly closer." God isn't waiting for you to get perfect before He can use you. Otherwise He wouldn't use anybody – ever. Someone said, "It takes fifteen years to become an overnight success."

Max Lucado, "When Grace happens" (2012)

Perhaps you were underestimated

Responding to jealousy was further unconscious preparation for David. His own brothers were jealous of him. How you respond to another's jealousy will determine whether you will truly come through as tomorrow's man or woman servant. For it is certain that it is only a matter of time before people will become jealous of your anointing. Perhaps you were underestimated by a perfectionist parent. Perhaps a brother or sister has been jealous of you; such is the stuff of life. All this gets you ready for the battle ahead. *"David behaved himself wisely in all his ways."* (I Sam.18:14) When you know someone is jealous of you, you will have to be extremely shrewd. You never let them know you know what their problem is.

*Do's and Don'ts Testing of Tomorrow's Man or Woman Servant Leaders

There are several do's and don'ts of which tomorrow's man or woman servant leader should be aware. Among which are:

- Don't grieve the Holy Spirit - The Holy Spirit is a person who can be grieved. *"Do not grieve the Holy Spirit of God, with whom you were sealed for the day of redemption."* (Eph.4:30) You may unconsciously grieve him by holding a grudge, a curt, flippant remark, a tongue that hurts another's credibility, etc. The chief way one grieves the Holy Spirit is by bitterness. Tomorrow's man or woman servant leader will have the ability to recognize the Holy Spirit and sense the things that grieve Him. An intimacy must be developed with Him that will enable you not only to tell what grieves Him but when, where and why it happens.

- Don't Vindicate Self - David was given the chance to kill King Saul, but he refused, thereby passing the self-vindication test. *"David said to Abishai, Don't destroy him! Who can lay a hand on the LORD's anointed and be guiltless?"*
 (I Sam 26:9) Every servant of God must pass this test, and all will be tested! Vindication belongs to God. It is written, *"To me belongeth vengeance, and recompence."* (Deut. 32:35)
 * *(Listing taken from R.T. Kendall's section on "Testing of Tomorrow's Man")*

Every servant of God, if honest, can testify to God's gracious intervention that keeps him or her from grievous sins. You don't usually know that you are being tested and that God and His angels are watching. Whether it is harboring a grudge, sexual temptation or vindicating ourselves, what seems like a satanic trap can be God's setup.

> *There hath no temptation taken you but such as is common to man: but God is faithful, who will not suffer you to be tempted above that ye are able; but will with the temptation also make a way to escape, that ye may be able to bear it.*
> *I Cor. 10:13*

*Openness To The Word and Holy Spirit
- Don't be uneasy when a person is giving a prophetic word of knowledge.
- Don't Fear manifestations of the Holy Spirit.
- Don't assume you are open to the Spirit today just because you were open yesterday.
- Don't assume you are open to the Spirit because God is blessing you.
- Do be open to the truth that you do not have everything and don't know everything.
- Do have a conscious desire to hear from God wherever He is and to recognize His movement.
- Do be sure there is no unconfessed sin.
- Do be sue there is no harboring of grudges or bitterness.
- Do walk in the light of God.
- Do be sure you have a life of prayer and Bible study.

*(Listing taken from R. T. Kendall's section "Openness to the Holy Spirit")

Open and obedience to the Spirit is gained by submitting to the bitting process

Tomorrow's anointing will result in being open to a combination of the Word and the Holy Spirit. The preparation aim of God for Tomorrow's Man or Woman servant leader is to make him or her open and obedient to the Spirit, which is gained by submitting to the bitting process.

As you open your heart to the move of God, ask Him for a deeper grasp of His Word. The Holy Spirit's anointing on you as Tomorrow's Man or Woman will have life-changing power. You will experience God's anointing showering upon you in ways that you've never imagined.

The Holy Spirit may not move on tomorrow's generation as He moved in our parent's, grandparent's, or in our generation, but He still moves. When you open up yourself to the Spirit you will recognize Him at work, and you will be at peace within yourself.

CHAPTER TWENTY-ONE
YESTERDAY'S SERVANT LEADER

Yesterday's Anointing

The anointing is when the Holy Spirit comes down on you. As stated before, it is a gift that functions easily when it is working. You cannot turn it on and you cannot turn it off.

> *The wind bloweth where it listeth, and thou hearest the sound thereof, but canst not tell whence it cometh, and whither it goeth: so is every one that is born of the Spirit.*
> *John 3:8*

When the anointing of the Holy Spirit is allowed to take over, He is no respecter of person. He may fall on laymen as well as clergy. Those who are called to serve the Lord as laymen have as much a high and noble calling as their brothers and sisters in the clergy. They are not second-class citizens.

No one can depend on education, culture or prestige to generate the Spirit's anointing. Anyone can train (and training is good), but only God calls and anoints people to spiritual leadership. A person's "gentle" upbringing counts for nothing. He or she may read dozens of books (but the Bible), attend countless management seminars, and take countless leadership courses, but unless they continually seek the Lord, their whole life and ministry will be marked with Yesterday's Anointing.

There is a fresh anointing for today

We risk the anointing and quench the Holy Spirit by allowing our education, culture and refinement to stand in the way. When this happens, some slip into yesterday's anointing by mimicking what once was when God's glory was present. They "work it up" – creating the shouting and manifestations that become pale imitations. Those who "work it up" as R. T. Kendall puts it are trying to box God into a certain way of manifesting His Spirit. They are trying to relive the glorious movements of yesterday. However, no matter how glorious God's Holy Spirit moved yesterday, there *IS* (emphasis added) a fresh anointing for today.

No one, no matter how gifted, can make yesterday's anointing be today's anointing if God is not in it. God does not always repeat Himself when manifesting His anointing.

Because the gifts and calling of God are irrevocable, a person can fall into the temptations of sin and still have a functional gift. God will not withdraw the gift simply because of the person's sin. He will not withdraw the gift because of faking in order to get results from "once had" anointing. But in the Day of Judgment, when the sheep are separated from the goats, those who have been, disobedient, disloyal and downright sinful will hear *"depart from me, I know you not."* Saul was anointed to be king over the children of Israel, but was later rejected by God because of his disobedience. He maintained his kingship, but under yesterday's anointing. He had become yesterday's man.

Study and hard work will always improve on your gifts. After all, we should *"Study to show ourselves approved"* – and this next part is key, *"unto God"* and not unto ourselves. There should be no boasting. Without a fresh anointing that only comes from having an intimate relationship with God, you can easily slip and fall into being Yesterday's Man or Woman.

Yesterday's Man or Woman servant has ceased to be relevant because of a failure to maintain a relationship with God. He or she is equivalent to a person trying to ride public transportation today with a "token" instead of a metro card. Such a person is completely out of touch with the MTA current travel currency. So it is with those saying the same things they have uttered in previous years to a new generation. To tell this generation to be sure not to leave home without tokens would evoke a response of perplexity.

The Three Be's

In order to avoid becoming Yesterday's Man or Woman servant leader, you must maintain an intimate and open relationship with God. Set a regular time each day to be alone with Him. If a man or woman is to be used of God his or her life must be lived in the secret place of intimate communion with Christ. His or her source of guidance, wisdom, strength to endure and spiritual power to achieve comes from God alone.

- Be sensitive to His Will – God's secret will refers to direct guidance.
  *Some basic questions that will guide you in seeking His will are:
- What does God want me to do today?
- Whom should I marry?
- Where should I go to church?
- Will I get this job?
- Should I move to a new neighborhood?

*List taken from R. T. Kendall's section "Am I Open To The Word?" There are many other questions not included here that you should ask.

> *In all thy ways acknowledge Him and He shall direct thy paths.*
> *Prov. 3:6*

- Be open to His Word – You are to prove yourself open to the Word by knowing what you believe. *"That we henceforth be no more children, tossed to and fro, and carried about with every wind of doctrine, by the sleight of men, and cunning craftiness, whereby they lie in wait to deceive."* (Eph. 4:14)

You must not deceive, neither should you be deceived.

- Be open to His Holy Spirit – Openness to the Holy Spirit is what will keep you in good standing and cause you not miss what God is in today. Although the Holy Spirit is as Jesus, the same yesterday, today and forever, and unchanging in nature, He does not always reveal Himself in one generation as He did in another. Don't risk missing the way in which God sovereignly chooses to manifest His glory. Stay spiritually current!

You must remain open to God's Word. You must remain open to the moving of His Spirit. You must *NOT* (emphasis added) become Yesterday's Man or Woman servant leader. Forsake not the spiritual bitting, again I say forsake it not!

www.ingramcontent.com/pod-product-compliance
Lightning Source LLC
Chambersburg PA
CBHW021146080526
44588CB00008B/238